C000262415

The Modern Witch's Book of

HOME REMEDIES

Sarah Lyddon Morrison

A Citadel Press Book
Published by Carol Publishing Group

Copyright © 1991 by Sarah Lyddon Morrison

A Citadel Press Book
Published by Carol Publishing Group
Citadel Press is a registered trademark of Carol Communications, Inc.

Editorial Offices   Sales & Distribution Offices
600 Madison Avenue   120 Enterprise Avenue
New York, NY 10022   Secaucus, NJ 07094

In Canada: Musson Book Company
A division of General Publishing Co. Limited
Don Mills, Ontario M3B 2T6

All rights reserved. No part of this book
may be reproduced in any form, except by
a newspaper or magazine reviewer who
wishes to quote brief passages in
connection with a review.

Queries regarding rights and permissions
should be addressed to: Carol Publishing Group,
600 Madison Avenue, New York, NY 10022

Manufactured in the United States of America
10 9 8 7 6 5 4 3 2 1

Carol Publishing Group books are available at special discounts
for bulk purchases, for sales promotions, fund raising, or
educational purposes. Special editions can also be created to
specifications. For details contact: Special Sales Department,
Carol Publishing Group, 120 Enterprise Ave., Secaucus, NJ 07094

Library of Congress Cataloging-in-Publication Data

Morrison, Sarah Lyddon.
    The modern witch's book of home remedies / Sarah Lyddon Morrison.
      p.   cm.
    "A Citadel Press book."
    ISBN 0-8065-1265-2
      1. Medicine, Popular. 2. Witchcraft. I. Title.
RC81.M89   1991
615.8'8—dc20   91-30768
                                                CIP

The Modern Witch's Book of

HOME
REMEDIES

To James Butler, that always savvy and knowledgeable Indian lore lover, who is my most beloved companion.

Contents

Acknowledgments

My personal thanks to Marsha Alvarez of the U.S. Public Health Service for providing me with raw data on which to base this book.

Also I would like to thank Mr. Richard Maybey for letting me use material from his book, *The New Age Herbalist*, Collier Books, Macmillan Publishing Company, 1988.

Introduction

Witches through the ages have enjoyed various kinds of celebrity. Sometimes they've been regarded as integral parts of the community, while in other ages, they've been thought of as evil and burned at the stake.

Modern witches are far from the days of torture, but we're still regarded with suspicion by some folks and accepted by others. Nothing much has changed in the way of other's attitudes toward us. But *we* know we're good witches with love spells and healing on our minds, and that's what really counts.

This book is designed to give you an idea of the kinds of remedies you can make to heal a variety of illnesses. They're all tested remedies and they're currently in use. I've gathered them in one book so that you won't have to hunt through the literature to find them. The remedies are herbal and you may wish to learn to grow your own herbs to make them. The art of healing is part of the history of witchcraft, so we must carry it on.

To properly use the herbs I mention, you'll need to know how to prepare them. What follows are instructions that I'll mention in the herb remedy pages by their name. If you memorize these instructions, you'll know what I'm talking about when I mention them in the recipes.

Infusion

To make an infusion, simply take boiling water and pour it over the green parts of the herb you're using. Make several cups and keep the infusion in a tight jar. It's best to use a glass pot to make the infusion and before you use it, strain it into a glass. If you're curing a cold, take the infusion boiling hot—but not more than four cups a day.

Decoction

This method of extraction, which is to remove the medicine from roots and other woody substances, requires boiling the barks, etc., in a glass pot for about ten minutes, then straining them into a covered jar. If there are green parts with the wood, boil these, starting with cold water. Make about two cups of decoction, and store it and use as you would an infusion.

Extract

Use about twice as much plant or herb to a few cups of water as you do for infusions. Keep the water cold and in a glass pot. Let the vegetable matter sit in the water for the day before straining and using it.

Juice

This is an easy method where you extract the vital juices from the plant by squeezing in an orange juice maker. Add water to the juice material and keep pressing till it runs dry. Juice should be taken right away so it won't lose its potency.

Dried Plants

Take the dried herb and crush it with mortar and pestle until fine. Take about an eighth of a teaspoon and use with water and something sweet if you like.

Ointment

Mix one part of your powder with three parts petroleum jelly after you've heated and melted it. When thoroughly mixed and cooled, the ointment can be used on your skin.

Poultice

Boil herbs or bark. Then either wrap the bark around the spot you're treating, or dip a cloth in the liquid and put it around the sore. Poultices are good for chest complaints or sores or bites and other intrusions on the limbs.

The Modern Witch's Book of

HOME
REMEDIES

I

Treatments for Common Illnesses

Common Colds

One of the nicest ways to treat a cold is to prepare an herbal bath to sit in or recommend to others if you feel expert enough as a witch to do some healing.

A bath made of ground mustard, which you boil in a decoction and soak your feet in, makes a soothing remedy for a cold or mild flu. Put the mustard in a bag made of old sheet, and boil it. You may wish to put the bag in a footbath to get even more of the remedy in the water. If you want to make a full bath of the mustard, use as much as a pound of the substance to make the decoction.

Another excellent way to treat a cold combines a vaporizer made out of a pot and blankets which cover you head to toe. You may use chamomile (six ounces of the flowers) boiled in a decoction to use beneath the blankets as a vapor treatment. Chamomile is also good for the nerves so it may have a calming effect as well as being soothing for colds or mild flu.

If you want to take something to drink for your cold or mild flu, then you might take a small bit of white pine bark and let

1

it steep in a cup or two of water. You need to use the inner bark of the white pine, or perhaps some new shoots to gather the resulting potion. Take the drink a mouthful at a time over a period of an hour or two. Be careful not to take too much of the potion or it may make you nauseous. Ask a doctor before taking this or any other potion internally.

Another drinkable potion is made with anise seed and one to three parts water which you boil. Then let the anise steep until cool. It will yield a very viable drink for chest colds, but you shouldn't take more than one cup in eight hours.

There are really hundreds of herbs that can be made into decoctions for use in vapor baths and teas to treat colds. Peppermint is a fine remedy, and can be boiled into a flavorful tea. Rose tea is another familiar remedy, and rosehip tea can be purchased at some old-fashioned emporia in the countryside. One of my favorite memories was coming upon such an all-purpose store along a country lane where a few houses were gathered. The store carried old-fashioned candy and aprons like grandmother used to wear, and had just everything that I recalled from childhood as being used by the elder members of the family. Rosehip tea was sold there, of course.

Another remedy from my childhood was to take hollyhock flowers and steep them as a tea. This is good for your throat as well as for a cold. And you have the fragrance of the hollyhock to comfort you while in bed.

Ginger is another way to treat a cold by boiling the root in a glass pan and drinking the mixture after it's cooled off. Most of these teas should be made in amounts of one- to one-and-a-half cups of water, which means you should have on hand good supplies of the roots and herbs. It's best to grow your own herbs, of course, but it's not always practical. You may have to write away for some ingredients or, best of all, go to a health food store to see what's available. You'd be surprised how many remedies can be found quickly in such shops.

The tasty fig turns out to be, in a decoction, a tea that is effective for colds and mild flu. It soothes the membranes in the throat and is tasty as well. Steep half a dozen figs in water for a tea, drink it, and you'll soon feel better.

For a very bad cough, the key is to take wild cherry bark and boil it for ten minutes, then let it stand before drinking. A cup of this mixture should be taken in the morning and the evening, but not more often. You may also use licorice for this tea, and in either case, the potent mixture should bring relief.

Sage or lungwort may be used for getting rid of bronchial cough. Make teas of these two, boiling for ten minutes each, and using parsimoniously throughout the day. You never want to overdo these healing teas, but take as little as possible to do the job.

Lemon, as every grandmother used to know, was an excellent remedy for coughs. Just boil lemon in water and take the tea to soothe your throat. You can safely make lemon tea, or these other recommended teas for your friends.

Peppermint tea is another old-fashioned standby. You may take peppermint leaves and make the tea, boiling for two or three minutes. You might even make mint juleps which will include heated liquor to soothe the cold.

Horehound also makes a fine tea as well as tasty candies. Use on bad colds to loosen the phlegm and give you a pleasant uplift.

Sage is yet another fine remedy for the common cold. Make a tea and take it twice a day. It's better to use fresh sage than the powdered variety, so pay a visit to your health food store if you haven't grown some for such occasions.

Another lovely-sounding remedy is sarsparilla, a favorite soft drink around the turn of the century. Make a tea and enjoy the flavorful aroma while it's steeping in the pot.

Almonds make a fine tea remedy for a cough and cold, and you can have two cups of this a day. Almond is also good for the skin or the face. But its sedative qualities make it most appealing for a cough you may have from smoking or a cold.

To help soothe your sore throat, you can make a mixture of rose petals and honey. It's the flowers and the hips that contain the medicine so use them in your cold remedy.

Balm of Gilead is actually another name for the popular tree and its medicinal properties. It's the balsam poplar to be exact and grows along the highways in Canada and the East Coast. You use the buds of the tree and turn the concoction into a vapor which you inhale from beneath a cosy tent of blankets. It's an expectorant, so you should take paper tissues with you under your vapor tent.

You should get some lungwort if you have a problem with coughing and a cold. Make it into a tea using boiling water, and take the mixture, after it cools, no more than twice a day. This remedy is also suggested for bronchitis, but if you know anything about bronchitis, it needs to be treated by a doctor, not just with a soothing herbal tea. It's very important to use these herbal remedies judiciously. A doctor's remedies, however, may be needed to take care of a lot of these complaints. I would never let bronchitis go with herbal attentions, because you so easily can develop pneumonia and then what do you have—a possible hospitalization. So be very careful, as I am, both in recommending to others or taking for yourself remedies for truly injurious conditions. You need to use common sense when dealing with the healing arts.

Another thing to bear in mind when making herbal teas and using other formulas for curing: these medications are powerful and may interact with the medications you've been given by your doctor. Take special care if you are administering remedies to others whose medical history you really don't know. I will try to point out when the teas are dangerous to use so that you won't commit homicide or suicide with your good intentions.

Aches

Agrimony is an herb that can be turned into a bath or poultice by making a decoction. Boil four of the dried leaves of the agrimony in one quart of water and then either enjoy the feeling of aches fading away in a bath, or wrap the decoction in pads of cloth around your feet and legs. This is a fine medication when taken externally. It's soothing and you should feel better quickly.

Knobgrass is another very good remedy for aches and pains. You should apply the leaves directly to your legs and feet, and if you have a bruise or another contusion, the herbs helps them to heal. So it's fine poultice to use.

Allspice, which may be found fresh in Caribbean-style botanicas in New York and elsewhere where there's a large population of Caribbean peoples, is excellent for alleviating aches and pains. It is said to have properties that make it anesthetic in a bath. Take some of the allspice—a few nuggets—and grind into a fine mash. Add to bathwater and see if your body doesn't relax right away. This is an especially welcome end-of-the-day refresher if you're not taking alcohol these days.

Other herbs that may be used in baths are especially helpful to any aches you may feel as a result of being tired. You may want the effect of the bath to be astringent so that you can pop out of the bath ready for a lively evening of dancing. If you feel the need for this type of bath, or have in mind some-one you want to stimulate as well, try adding strawberry root, mixed with some of its leaves, and feel how springy you are right away.

Sage is another plant that will stir your tired blood to action. Add a handful of fresh sage leaves to your bathwater for the desired effect.

If you want the opposite effect to take place, and wish to spend the evening sleeping in your perfumed bed, then have a bath with marjoram leaves in it. Stretch out in the tub with a candle and book of love poems and just relax. Passion flower will have the same effect as the marjoram, so you can change the perfume of your herbal baths occasionally.

If you have a cat that sometimes scratches you, you can soothe your skin by adding peppermint to your bath. You can use oil of peppermint, or the leaves of the herb. Besides being soothing, peppermint is one of the antiseptic herbs that's good for your skin and small scratches and other contusions you have.

Chamomile flowers, which are easy to find in any health food store, can be used in a bath as an antiseptic. They are just about the best all-purpose herbal remedy I know, and chamomile is used for a wide variety of ailments. A package of chamomile flowers given as Christmas gifts to all your "patients" whom, as a healing witch, you've acquired, are just the ticket.

Allergies

You may wish to make teas to ease allergies that you may have, so think about making dandelion tea like your grandmother gave you as a child for ailments. But don't do it. Dandelion can cause people with allergies to the weed to break out with time, and cause needless pain and a trip to the doctor. Instead, try the following ingredients to make a tea that should be drunk no more than twice a day. Take honeycomb, apple cider vinegar, and ginseng and make a concoction that will soothe not only your spirits but hives if you break out with them.

Anemia

You should be interested to learn that a fine remedy for anemia is artichoke. Boil the plant in a glass container and then enjoy the artichoke as you would ordinarily.

Another very good remedy is chive. Take the herb and make tea with it—enough for two cups in one day.

Dandelion tea is another cure for anemia, and my mother made it for us as kids. It tastes somewhat bitter, but you can always add honey to it.

Comfrey, still another well-known healing herb, makes wonderful tea for other reasons beyond anemia. So you can't go wrong with that.

Aphrodisiac

Rosebuds are recommended as an aphrodisiac tea as well as sweet-smelling additives to your bed. Aroma-therapy relies heavily on rose petals, buds, flowers, and hips to make one as well as one's surroundings sweet-smelling. To make the rosebud tea, put two tablespoons of buds in boiling water. Steep for fifteen minutes and add honey or other sweetener to the tea. Drink leisurely and get yourself in the mood for luxurious lovemaking.

Valerian in bath water makes an excellent aphrodisiac stimulant. You should add one part valerian to four parts water which you bring to a boil and then put the concoction in your bath water. You may also do the same with pansies which you may pick from your garden. Add some pansy flowers to your tub and let them float about you while you and your lover enjoy the bath together. Candles and a bouquet of flowers from your garden should complete the aprhodisiac bath.

Asthma

One of the nicest ways to treat asthma is with an herbal bath. Put half a pound of ground mustard in a muslin bag and boil it for ten minutes. Then put the mustard in your bath and sit back and relax and inhale the healing mustard herb. It should open your breathing passages so you won't have such a hard time with the asthmatic condition. Enjoy the bath for a half hour or so and then climb into bed for the night, confident that you won't be kept from sleep by the asthma.

Baths

Some of the following baths will calm you, others will make your skin tingle, and still more will smooth your skin like body cream. For any of the baths, just boil a handful of the herb in water while the herb is inside a cloth bag. Then put the water and herb bag in your bathtub. The aromatic herbs will relax you and you'll feel like a new person after your bath.

For a bath to set your skin tingling, take sage, comfrey root, and strawberry root, as I've mentioned, put them in a cloth bag and into your tub. You will feel wide awake. The best time for this bath is after a long day at the office when you have a party to go to in the evening and want to feel revived.

For a very calming bath when you want to return to serenity after being upset by what someone has said or done to you, take a handful of valerian, marjoram, and passion flower and put them in a cloth bag. A half-hour bath will have you ready to go again or, better, be ready for bed. Always take your baths late in the day for full effect.

For a bath that promotes good health if you've recently

been sick with a sore throat or flu, try milfoil, chamomile, and rosemary in a little bag to add to your bath. If you don't want to go through all the trouble of making a decoction, it's perfectly all right to just put the bag in the warm tub with you. You won't have quite the effect of boiling the herbs first, but if you just don't feel up to it, just drop the bag in the bath water.

Instead of using bath oil or bubble bath in your tub, why not try an herbal remedy which will leave your skin baby-soft and glowing? Put together in a muslin bag handfuls of orange blossoms, rosehips, rose petals, and chamomile flowers, and boil them together before putting the mixture in the bathtub itself. Your skin will become silky with herbs and the aroma from the mixture will fill your house with the scents of romance.

To soothe tired feet and muscles after a long day, you might try a bath filled with the intoxicating scents of thyme, rosemary, lavender, and peppermint. You should feel rejuvenated and able to spring from your tub a new person. You might further relax yourself with a glass of champagne while· lolling in your tub, and if you fit your lover in, too, then the world will turn rosy and all cares will leave you.

Another remedy for smoothing your skin and soothing your soul is made of small handfuls of buttercups, chervil, cucumber, and primrose. Blend these flowers and herbs in a muslin bag and let them boil for about ten minutes. Before putting them in the tub, you can also make a poultice for your feet or whatever else aches, and let your sore body sit for a few minutes with the poultice in place. Put the water and bag in your bath and, after first testing the heat of the water, jump in and enjoy. You will feel double pampered after this treatment.

Violets, heather, juniper, and lemon also make a lovely nosegay of scents for your bath. These will smooth your skin and act as a tonic to your tired body after a long day at work. Often there are parties right after work that you must attend for your career's sake, and you can take a few minutes in the ladies room with your herbs. You can heat the herbs under the tap, then rub them gently around and over your throat and face, and a new application of makeup will make your face glow.

Another bath that treats your skin and makes you refreshed and able to nimbly get through your day or evening features olive, pansy, and papaya, which, when mixed together, is a soothing balm for your bathwater treatment. The papaya, especially, is used in the Caribbean where it grows wild, and if you vacation there, plan to bring some root stock back so you can have your own supply grown indoors.

Watercress, white pond lily, and wild clover make a romantic combination to soak in. Choose this bath for your skin's rejuvenation in summer where you have access to clover and pond lilies and can make a truly romantic combination with watercress in a bath for you and your lover. Recommend this bath to friends who come to you with questions about healing baths, and they'll be forever grateful.

Wild strawberry (which may be picked in the early summer in the Eastern states), willow, and wintergreen make a stimulating bath. Most herb or health food stores carry these and other combinations for baths to soften your skin. Take a look around and make your own combinations.

Blood Pressure

If your blood pressure is either too high or too low, garlic and ginger will help stabilize it. For low blood pressure, you might also try anise, heather, lavender, and rosemary. And for high blood pressure, in addition to whatever the doctor prescribes, take chervil, onion, parsley, and rue. It's very important to take the medication prescribed for blood pressure conditions, as not properly taking care of yourself may lead to a stroke. Wild black cherry is also recommended for blood pressure that's too high. You might feel comfortable talking to your doctor about herbal remedies in addition to medication you take to see if they're in harmony. You don't want to take something that will conflict with your modern medications.

Childbirth

To ease your body after childbirth, make a poultice of birthwort, flax, cotton, and pansy. Lay it cross your distended stomach and wait for the soothing effect of the herbs and fibers. You may also make a poultice of shepherd's purse, silverweed, and wild red raspberry that is especially comforting to tired legs at the end of the day. Don't use these poultices unless you're absolutely in need of them while you're pregnant, because you want your pregnancy to be as free from any kind of drug assistance as possible. The old fashioned way that people like my mother used in the matter of pregnancy was to take all foods in moderation and stay away from cigarettes, alcohol, or any other mood-altering substances. Mother believed in natural childbirth and had all three of her children at home. We were definitely the product of the best sort of beginning one could wish for, and young mothers today should strive for the kind of birthing ideals that women of my mother's generation did.

Colds (More Remedies)

There are other cold remedies that soothe and make the symptoms of the common cold less annoying. Among these are teas made with anise, barley water, cinnamon, garlic, ginseng, honey, lemon, peppermint, and mustard. None of these remedies is harmful unless taken in excessive doses, so if you brew tea from any of them, be sure it's only in moderation. Ginseng, I understand, today is sold in a much milder form than it was twenty years ago, but always check your herbs to make certain they aren't so powerful as to make you ill.

Other remedies for coughs and heavy colds are almond, camphor, garlic, horehound, lemon, limeflowers, licorice, peppermint, and wintergreen. Teas can be made of these, and two cups a day are sufficient for remedy. There are no Food and Drug Administration approvals on herb teas that are sold in health food stores, so you're on your own when you use herbs, whether picked from your garden or the woods or bought in the stores. That's why it's always best to take a moderate dosage of herbs so that you won't do damage to yourself. A number of herbs are the cause of vomiting and diarrhea if taken in too powerful a dosage, and can be even more harmful than that. In this book, I won't list herbs that are really poisonous, so you can sample some of these remedies knowing that they aren't altogether dangerous. But you must always be wary when you put something in your mouth that it will not harm you.

Constipation

While over-the-counter laxatives are in wide use and are effective, you may wish to try or recommend to a friend an herbal treatment. Apple, clove, figs, honey, licorice, prunes, and spinach are all touted as laxatives and will do the job well. I always eat three prunes in the morning to make sure I won't get constipated and the treatment works. My father doted on licorice for the same reasons. Go ahead and try one of these remedies and see if they don't work.

Cramps

If you have cramps in your legs or other parts of your body, you might remedy them with a tea made from peppermint or eucalyptus. Put a dash of vinegar in the tea, and some honey, if you like, and your cramping should ease. Don't try to treat with teas stomach cramps that persist. See a doctor. But the tea would be very soothing if the cramps are menstrual.

Dandruff

The little white flakes that indicate dandruff can be swept away with home remedies for them. Chamomile tea can help control dandruff as can such treatments as English elm, English walnut, and olive. These three woods, when boiled and rendered of their pulp, can be smoothed on the hair and left to do their work for fifteen minutes and then soaked away. Rosemary and willow provide another good remedy when applied directly to the scalp. Several weeks' worth of treatments should render dandruff completely harmless and gone.

Diarrhea

Make a tea if you're having a lot of diarrhea and don't want to control it with an over-the-counter drug. You may use barley, blackberry, peppermint, or rice, and soothe your stomach and intestines till they stop acting up. If you're having a lot of gas with your condition, you might wish to have a tea of cinnamon, clove, dill, ginger, nutmeg, or fennel. All of these will help flatulence and excessive gas that comes as part of the diarrhea.

Diuretic

Don't supplement, with these foods, the need for a good diuretic prescribed by your doctor for high blood pressure or other conditions. Use the foods if you feel bloated because of your period, or some other mild state of discomfort. Apples, celery, grapes, onions, and parsley all have a mildly diuretic effect and you may wish to add them to your diet to deal with too much water in your body.

Ears

If you have a slight earache and you're pretty certain that it isn't an infection, then you might try a remedy of caraway or chamomile tea to see if that doesn't do the trick. Eating garlic may also help, as may onion and yarrow. But as I said, if it's an infection, see a doctor immediately before the ache becomes too painful. Don't ever give children home remedies without consulting a physician because earaches are quite often infections that need to be handled with modern medicine.

Eczema

There is still room in the treatment of eczema for home remedies to be used. Aloe vera, a known healing plant, is a fine remedy. Grow the plant in your house, and when you have eczema, pinch a leaf off the plant and rub the juice right on the condition. Aloe vera is also good for burns that you may get around a stove or iron. Follow the same procedure of pinching off a leaf for the juices within which go directly on the burn. You may also try blackberry leaf, a poultice of oatmeal, or artichokes. These should be used in conjunction with appropriate medication for the skin condition.

Eyes

While there's no real way to change short-sightedness or any other condition of the eyes that requires wearing glasses, the following may also help you find improvement in your vision. Eat an apple and some cabbage and cucumber in a salad and feel confident that you're indulging in the right foods for an eye condition. Rosewater, thyme, and fennel may also be used to assist in this matter. Carrots, of course, are a famous cure for a minor eye condition and I've been eating them since childhood in the hope they may cure my near-sightedness. Nothing, unfortunately, has helped and I must wear contact lenses. Also try a poultice to cover your eyes using oats, parsley, and plantain. These are soothing to the eyes and should be placed in a bag of muslin to cover them. If you're not allergic to dandelion tea, you might try some of this for eye conditions. But be very careful of dandelion because people are allergic to it and it can be a double-edged cure. Rue and savory are also herbs that can be used for the eyes. Put them in your food as spices and they will be beneficial to your condition.

Fever

If you have a slight fever with your cold or other mildly discomforting illness, then feed yourself apples, barley water, ginseng, and grapes as well as strawberries and lemons. These are all foods that help bring a fever back to normal. If you have a dangerously high temperature, then you should obviously see a doctor as these foods wouldn't do much good with a terrible condition. But with a mild fever, they help immensely.

Flu Stopper

Make a mixture of cayenne pepper, vinegar, a pinch of cinnamon, and licorice and drink the brew to keep from getting the flu. This preventative also can be used for keeping away colds, and if you're one of those people who regularly has a cold every spring and fall, this brew may do you some good.

Gastroenteritis

If you want to use home remedies on gastroenteritis, be sure to consult your doctor to make certain that none of your remedy ingredients conflict with medication given to you for your condition. If he says it's all right for you to medicate yourself, then try the following recipes. Use thyme, licorice, and oat with peppermint and plantain to make as a tea. Use one ingredient only in making the teas, but any of the above will be beneficial. These teas should soothe your condition and give you the desire to sleep, which is fine as you've probably been in some pain and need the rest.

Genital Infections

If you have a genital infection, head for the doctor and get the recommended creams and ointments as well as antibiotics if they are needed. Then you may wish to make celery tea or a sassafras tea, both of which are very efficacious for your condition. Eat parsley or make a wintergreen tea which will ease the situation. Indian corn makes another good remedy, so you've plenty of choices. Stay away from some of the fancier herbs (such as white pond lily or Queen of the Meadow) that might be good for the conditions because it isn't yet known what affect a combination of these herbs has with modern medicine. It could be unfortunate or just render useless the modern drugs you need to take. So stick with the lighter herbs that have a widespread reputation for not being harmful to you.

Gout

Here's a disease that needs to be treated with modern medicine but can benefit from some home remedy poultices as well. Take some horseradish, meadowsweet, and mountain holly and make a poultice for your legs as that's usually where gout strikes first. Sassafras tea is also good for gout, but again, you don't want to try too many teas in conjunction with what a doctor prescribes as the effects on each other are not known. Watercress is also good for gout, so you might try that without ill effect. The idea of the remedy is to ease the pain and swelling that gout entails. You might apply a poultice of oats as well, as it's very soothing. Willow and witch grass make another poultice that works well on gout, and if you live in Colorado, try some quaking aspen in a poultice to ease the swelling.

Gums

If you're looking for an unusual mouthwash beyond the confines of Scope and others of its breed, you'll want to take some blackberry, black currant, and watercress, boil them together, then let them cool before using. Just swish the concoction around in your mouth. Feel your breath changing from nighttime mouth to fresh and clean. For a fancier variety, use barberry, comfrey, and dogwood (be sure not to ingest these). I can't recommend swallowing the mouthwashes; just use them to freshen your breath.

Hair Care

To beautify your hair (remember the good old days when everybody was putting beer in their hair?), here are some potions to bring out the shine and make you look good. Make a tonic of vinegar (apple cider), rhubarb, and sage and see if you don't look your best.

Hair Tonics

These hair tonics don't return long-gone hair to your head. They're just for sweetening and freshening your hair, as a tonic will, and they make a nice change from the bottled kind you find at the drugstore. Burdock or black elder make potent tonics (mix with alcohol), and juniper and lavender are a sweet combination. Meadowsweet and nasturtium make fine tonics as do rosemary and sage. The recipe for making as tincture is to combine four ounces of powdered herb with twelve ounces alcohol to which you add water to make a fifty percent alcohol solution. You should let stand for two weeks, shake at least once a day, then strain and store the liquid in a tightly-lidded bottle. The tincture should last a long time. I wouldn't use the tonic more than every other day, as tinctures tend to be very strong versions of herbal remedies. You don't want to overdo.

Another sweet hair tonic is made from apple cider vinegar, rhubarb, and sage, mixed together as a tincture.

Headache

If you have a prolonged headache, or a migraine, see a doctor, as it may be a symptom of another illness far more serious than just a common headache. But if you know it's the type that aspirin would do away with and you don't want to take aspirin for it, then try one of these remedies. Take basil, cayenne pepper, ginger, and marjoram, and mix together in a tea. As it cools, take a few sips and see if the headache slowly disappears. Chamomile tea also works on headaches, and a combination of parsley, peppermint, rosemary, and sage will take away the pain. Garlic and lavender are also fine remedies. If your headache continues, it may be a migraine that you're familiar with and have gone to the doctor about. If your usual medication is not handy, try a tea of fennel or fragrant valerian and even hops. That should rid you of the pain.

Heart

After doing your exercises, you might want to take a tonic that's especially good for the heart. Cayenne pepper, cucumber, and garlic make a fine combination as a pick-me-up. Oat, onion, and primrose make another combination that will restore your heart to its normal beat. Wait, of course, till you're cooled down if you've been jogging or running, and don't take much of your tonic, just a few sips. It's better for you than Gatoraid or other soft drinks and you'll be able to recommend it to your friends who exercise as you do. Foods that go well with heart care are asparagus, wild cherry, garlic, onion, lemon juice, and rosemary. You can make these into a tonic or have them for lunch, whichever suits you.

Hemorrhoids

If you don't want to take the popular over-the-counter medications for hemorrhoids and your doctor hasn't prescribed any medication for your condition, then try a home remedy to see if it won't help you. Aloe is a good choice for the itching and burning of the hemorrhoids, as it works so well on skin burns. And the common plantain is another good bet, also from the Caribbean. Horse chestnut, closer to home, can be used as a balm for your painful condition. And lemon spread on the hemorrhoid should shrink it, as should witch hazel. Foods such as red potatoes should be eaten when you have hemorrhoids, and you can use cocoa butter to help with some of the itching and burning sensations. Bayberry is also a remedy but be careful of how much you use, as home remedies should be taken in small doses.

Hoarseness

Garden raspberries, black currants, blackberries, and okra are very fine for hoarseness. So is that old standby, lemon, which, it is said, the opera singers used to use before a performance if they had any hoarseness. Onions and plantain work on the throat, and sage and wild black cherry are also remedies. If you don't get relief from your hoarseness in a short while after gargling with the above remedies, then it may be that you've come under the spell of a witch and need to see one yourself to have the curse removed. It could be that someone close to you is jealous and managed to get hold of some of your hair to take to a witch who put on a spell to make you hoarse. If you sing for pleasure or a living, this is worse than death. If you don't do the above, then it's to annoy you.

Impotence, Frigidity

There are a lot more cases of sexual dysfunction around than anybody really knows about in the medical field. And not much can be done about the condition if it's chemically caused. Some medicines help for a short while and then seem to lose their power just like the condition. So you may wish to try—or recommend to friends who come to you with this problem—some home remedies that have just about as much chance of working as modern medical prescriptions. Asiatic ginseng is an old aphrodisiac, as well as three foods: celery, lettuce, and plantain. You should eat plenty of these foods when undergoing home remedy treatment. Onion, saffron, and savory are herbs that should be taken as teas to counteract the impotence or frigidity. English walnut can be used if carefully prepared. And, as always, you should check to see if you have any enemies who might have put a curse on you sexually. In addition, you should find out if the condition is psychological. If it isn't, then try the home remedies. You can consult Oriental material on the subject, as there are lots of interesting aphrodisiacs. Those listed here have a European heritage and are not as exotic on the subject of aphrodisiacs to benefit you.

Indigestion

Some people suffer from nervous stomach conditions that lead to indigestion. The reasons can be psychological or physical but upset stomach is the result. You may wish to make a tea of artichoke or even eat one, after carefully boiling it and draining the water you cooked it in. Artichoke is very soothing, but don't forget to take the choke out of it before using it. Chamomile is another soothing tea to take when having trouble with stomach upset. Chamomile can be used for a lot of ailments as it's such a calming herb. Coriander also may be used. Try to buy the green herb and make a tea of it. The same can be said of carraway, carrots, and comfrey which all make fine teas for indigestion.

My father had a nervous stomach and Mother was hard put to cook for him. In his later years, he was able only to eat small hamburger patties and potatoes. Everything else, especially fried foods, really upset his system. But on occasions when the family went out to a restaurant, he would not even think about his condition and ordered anything he felt like. I never saw him ill after that, so I wonder how much of his indigestion was psychological. We never did find out, however, as he was born in an era when resorting to psychologists and psychiatrists was not done. So he suffered through his life with a variety of psychologically brought on conditions. The worst was indigestion as it made him wholly unpleasant to be around. Mother tried hard to bring variety to his diet but her efforts seldom worked and she gave up and just cooked him hamburger patties.

Today such discomfort and suffering would be unthinkable over a long period of time. We'd find some way to alter the condition. But in the early part of the century, large families were "in" and doctors were not consulted as they are today. Medical problems facing people of that era were entirely different from ours because so many conditions could lead to death without proper medication. Bronchitis could become pneumonia, a common way to die. I've had bronchitis dozens of times, taken care of it right away and lived to see another day. Such serious disease should be treated with modern medicine because home remedies don't work on an illness such as pneumonia. If you live in a woodsy environment, you might argue that the herbs you use do cure pneumonia among other serious ailments, but city dwellers who aren't familiar with what roots grow in the woods and countryside shouldn't try to medicate themselves without a thorough knowledge of how to use the home remedies. Dandelion tea (if you're not allergic to it) can be used to remedy indigestion, as well as garlic, either taken whole or made into a soup or even tea. Horseradish is also recommended for an upset stomach and, while I've never used it, you might try a bit of lavender. Be especially careful of unknown remedies. Oats and orange may be used to make teas that are wonderful on an upset stomach. In fact the whole gamut of edible herbs that I recommend can be used for indigestion. There's papaya, parsley, peppermint, rhubarb, rosemary, saffron, sage, star anise, sweet marjoram, white mustard, while black cherry, and winter savory. Anything you put in your stomach, you want to be sure is edible. There are a number of poisonous herbs that if used will make you violently sick.

Inflammation

If some part of your skin is inflamed for any reason, perhaps through an infection that you didn't treat with iodine, then do so by all means and also make a home remedy to help the speed of recovery. Apply to the inflammation comfrey, vinegar, and witch hazel. You may choose among these remedies or use one or two in conjunction with each other.

Itching

There are a number of over-the-counter medications for itching but you might try a home remedy too if it persists. Apply apple cider vinegar, anise, juniper, lemon juice, oatmeal, and some yogurt. You can use one or two of the remedies, and if they are successful, try another if the itching persists. Be careful and mindful of itching if it comes from warts, for example, as it may indicate that your wart is changing and you need to see a doctor to have it removed.

Insect Bites

Recipes for home remedies for bites are for those of insects such as mosquitoes and not for poisonous snakes and the like. For those, unless you're an expert at handling them, you must go immediately to a doctor or hospital and hope they have an antidote. I was taught as a child, growing up in a place where no poisonous snakes lived, to take a knife and cut slits around the bite, then suck the blood until the poison was gone. But those days for such home remedies are gone, and the recommended procedure is to go to a medical facility. But if you've received bites from mosquitoes or other small insects, then you can safely use a home remedy to stop the itching. Aloe is recommended. Take a leaf and squeeze the healing plant milk onto the itchy bite. This should help you feel better fast. We used to use calamine lotion for a particular tiny bite, and I'm sure it still works well today. Calamine is sort of an all-purpose remedy purchased over-the-counter and it's especially useful if you've got some poison ivy and don't want to spread it to other parts of your body. Witch hazel is another rub-on remedy which can make you feel much better in a short time. And if you want to use mint for a poultice then expect it to work quickly. Leek may be used and wild hyssop is a remedy. Olive and parsley are other remedies and the leaves of the goldenrod (if you're not allergic) may be used in a poultice to stop the itching.

Insomnia

Chamomile is a very soothing tea to take to put you to sleep if you're having trouble in that area. And a magical remedy is to take garden violet, put it in a silver bag under your pillow, and then lay back and wait for the desired effect: sleep. Dill and dandelion also work on insomnia. Orange and passion flower are other plants that take away the sleeplessness you experience. Primrose and rosemary also may be used in a tea to take away your insomnia but I prefer that you put shavings from a white birch into a white muslin bag and wear it around your neck. You should doze off almost immediately. Wild marjoram and sweet marjoram may be made into teas, too, and you may wish to make a poultice of lettuce and hops and mother of thyme to cover your eyes. Sleep should be induced soon after applying it.

Joints

If your joints are inflamed with arthritis or bursitis, you need to take medicine that is prescribed for you to dispel the pain of your condition. But you may also use poultices to keep your joints treated while waiting for the doctor's medication to work. Eucalyptus may be made into a poultice to wrap around your joints, and you may wish to add onion and vinegar to the decoction to insure that the pain will be removed.

Kidneys

If you're having minor kidney problems that don't require a trip to a physician, you may use home remedies to clear up the congestions or whatever is ailing you. Alfalfa is good if you make a decoction and drink it sparingly. Black currant will also do the trick in a tea form, and celery and cucumber eaten as a salad with parsley and asparagus and cayenne pepper should aid your condition. European goldenrod—use the leaves to make tea (don't use this weed if you're allergic to goldenrod)—can be relieving. Heather is also recommended but I'd rather you use it as a poultice over your liver. A touch of horseradish in your food will also aid in the healing of kidneys. So see a doctor and tell him which remedy you're taking so the medication prescribed won't conflict with your teas, herb poultices, etc.

Liver

If you have been drinking a lot, you need to spend some time considering the condition of your liver. Cirrhosis of the liver is the sign of the truly suffering alcoholic. So if you've been drinking, you should offer your liver a rest by giving it, among other things, a tonic. Artichoke is good for your liver, as well as apples, beets, asparagus, burdock, chicory, dandelion, peppermint, prune, garlic, oat, onion, radish, rosemary, and lemon juice. If you want to make tea with any of these foods, you may do that, or just eat them as ordinary fare. I once was told by a doctor that cirrhosis of the liver can take place after only one drink or thousands. You never know what kind of system you have until the alcohol causes damage. Take care of yourself and stick with the people who have given up drinking and smoking. They're the real role models for the nineties and good examples to those who haven't stopped being self-destructive.

Lungs

Lungs need to be coddled if you're a heavy smoker. You really need to beat the addiction before it interferes with your life by giving you lung cancer. You need to eat celery and sage in a tea and make poultices to lay across your chest over your lungs, of eucalyptus, comfrey and fenugreek. Ground ivy can be used, too, and Irish moss if you can get some. Kidney beans are good to eat, and milfoil with pansy makes a sweet-smelling poultice.

Menstruation

To take away some of the cramping and unpleasantness of menstruation, make a tea of parsley, saffron, and sage and enjoy the calming results. Chamomile tea is another standby recipe as is tea of wild marjoram. It's amazing that home remedies for a woman's menstrual period are still used when modern medicine fails to help. If the doctor prescribes something for you, call him before taking the home remedies to let him know what you're doing. It's possible that the teas may take away the effect of what he prescribed, or that the interaction of the medicine and tea is not a good one. So always tell your doctor if you're taking something besides what he prescribes. For excessive menstruation, you might try comfrey or wild strawberry. These herbs will often regulate the blood flow. Again, however, consult with your doctor. Other remedies include carrot, cayenne pepper, cinnamon bark, lemon juice, lentil, and red raspberry. You can make these into teas or just eat them as they are. They're helpful foods to eat in your condition.

If your menstruation is tardy, and you're certain you're not pregnant, then try carrot, celery, damask rose, chamomile, ginger, lovage, parsley, peppermint, rosemary, sage, tarragon, watercress, white mustard, or wild ginger. Any of these—or a discreet combination of a few of them—should help bring on your menstrual period. If these don't work as much as you think they should, check with the doctor as there may be something more serious than just a tardy menstrual period.

Milk

If you're a new mother, you may take home remedies to bring on the flow of milk and keep it strong. Anise and basil taken as a tea will promote milk, and caraway and dill will have the same effect. Fennel and hops make a fine remedy as do Iceland moss, parsley, sage, and wild raspberry. Make teas of these and you'll find your milk flowing regularly and when you need it.

Nausea, Vomiting

Usually nausea and vomiting indicate a serious problem that you should see a doctor about. But if you know what's causing the condition (drinking too much, for example), then you can try a home remedy on it. My personal recipe is fried egg sandwich and chocolate milk. This will immediately take away the symptoms of hangover from the night before. But if you prefer a tea, try anise and asparagus the morning after, or have a hair-of-the-dog, or barley and caraway. Another effective remedy is clove tea, being careful not to have more than two cups a day. Nothing is sweeter smelling and more restorative than a tea of clove. Chamomile, that old standby, is also good for nausea and vomiting, and ginger and ginseng are also prescribed for your condition. Hops, another hair-of-the-dog, makes a suitable remedy for too much beer, while peppermint, quaking aspen (if you have some in your yard), sage and savory, spearmint, and sweet marjoram, wild clover and raspberry, wild yam, and winter savory are all remedies for simple nausea and vomiting. As I have warned you, however, don't try to medicate yourself if you haven't been drinking and can't figure out what is making you sick. Always get medical advice if you have two or three conditions and you're not sure which remedy is the right one.

Nerves

If you have a nervous condition which is the result of neurosis, then you'll want something to calm you down and restore tranquility as soon as possible. There are many, many medications that doctors use for nervousness of all kinds, but you may still want to try a home remedy. Since pills for mental conditions are very powerful and can easily change in composition when crossed with other drugs, be sure that your psychiatrist knows what you're doing in the way of drinking teas, or whatever your decoctions are.

He may not even know the results of herb remedies with next-century-power drugs, you should consider not taking anything in the home remedy line. But if you're not taking the powerful mental drugs for your nerves, then, by all means, go ahead and try chamomile tea or teas made with cumin, clove, lavender, limeflowers, almond, celery, violets, hops, lettuce, olive, orange, pansy, passion flower, and rosemary. Herbs for nervous conditions are plentiful and just about any one of the herbs mentioned so far are used for one condition or another. But I swear by the old standby such as chamomile when nerves need to be unjangled. And just as the British do, you might try some plain teas, maybe jasmine or Earl Grey for a traditional method of curing nerves. Peppermint and rosemary also make fine teas and are recommended for nerves. But as I said, don't take any of these powerful remedies without first finding out if they might interfere with prescribed medication.

Neuralgia

If you have a sharp pain that radiates along your nerves, then you may be experiencing neuralgia. Of course, if the pain gets worse, you need to get some medical attention, otherwise you might try a home remedy for it. Allspice makes a pleasant tea that is good for this condition, and celery as well as chamomile and horse chestnut are also remedies. Wild marjoram and wild yam make delicious teas that can be helpful to pain that just caught you and horseradish, lemon, and peppermint also make fine remedies. But you have to know yourself and your aches and pains well enough to know when it's time to give up teas and go to the doctor. If you want to make a poultice to put on the pain, try willow or Queen of the Meadow or skullcap, which can be placed over the affected area and left on to soothe for ten minutes or so.

Night Sweats

These sweats are common among drinkers who wake up in the middle of the night bathed in perspiration. For getting drunk and doing the miserable things to yourself brought on by drinking, you should be thoroughly ashamed. But if you want to treat your sweats, especially if you haven't been drinking but have got them as a result of another condition, then try a poultice made of balm, English walnut, or French rose on your back. You can drink a tea made of hops if you think you can prepare that in the middle of the night. Or take some hyssop and sage with or without wild strawberry which can be fixed as a therapeutic tea by itself. Naturally, if you get night sweats constantly and don't drink, I think you should be concerned enough to at least place an inquiring phone call to your physician.

Obesity

Short of going in for an operation to get rid of fat (such as having your stomach stapled), there is no fast sure way to lose weight. So all the over-the-counter remedies have nothing over homemade ones. You can pick and choose your teas as you wish and, as long as you don't expect to lose thirty pounds in two weeks, you can gradually, pound by pound, week by week, get rid of unwanted fat. Apple is recommended both for eating and as a tea. And black currant also makes a delightful tea. That good old dieter's standby, celery, is recommended as a tea, and fennel makes a fine home remedy, too. Hops and Irish moss are remedies and sassafras as well as watercress and willow make fine teas. If you want to put a poultice on the area where you're trying to lose your most weight, then try common buckthorn, fig tree, ground ivy, and meadowsweet. Used singly or in combination, these make a fine poultice for your fat areas. I don't think anything can get rid of cellulite (in spite of the television advertisements) but you can at least try by putting poultices on those areas of your legs and stomach and upper arms to see if they do any good. And if one of these remedies or a combination of them actually work, then you can patent the poultice and make a fortune just as easily as others do now with lesser medications. But the old standby for losing weight is to just eat smaller amounts of food and try to keep on a strict one thousand calorie diet for however many weeks your doctor recommends and watch the results that way. Try this weight loss routine when you're young so you won't have to face a lifetime as an overweight adult.

So many doors are unfairly closed to the overweight in the job world and among people who choose not to be your friend if you're obese. I know because when I hit middle age, I put on the pounds as if by magic. Then I lost sixty pounds but decided to give up smoking. I put back twenty and became addicted to sugar, so I'm in the same predicament as before. But sometime this year I hope to conquer the sugar addiction and move on to losing those pounds again. If I can get my willpower revved up like I did when I chose to stop smoking, then I'm sure I'll win this battle. But it isn't easy and it isn't funny. It's very hard work and emotionally draining. Obesity is used in the job market to screen out candidates, and I know of one place that would only hire Miss Washington, D.C., types for reception and secretarial jobs even though the company was rarely visited by customers. It was just that the young guys running the place wanted to be surrounded by beautiful women. The world is a very cutthroat place for the heavy, and if not for your ego, you need to stay slender for your livelihood. Keep at it, and soothe yourself with some teas and poultices to keep the road from being overly bumpy!

Prostate

Anything unusual about the prostate should be immediately reported to the doctor as it could indicate cancer. Men develop cancer of the prostate at an alarming rate, and they have to be aware of it at all times. Just as breast cancer in women can be treated if detected early, so too with prostate. But you can use teas and poultices to soothe your organs. Garlic and horse chestnut make fine teas as well as parsley and rosemary. White pond lily can be used as a poultice, as can wintergreen and witch grass. Club moss can also be used as a poultice and saw palmetto if you live in southern climes. But if you do have something wrong with your prostate, be sure to tell the doctor treating you that you're drinking teas or using poultices so he can gauge the effect his prescribed medication has in conjunction with the home remedies. Some people are afraid to confide in their doctors, but they shouldn't be.

Rheumatism

If you have rheumatism, you can probably find relief in the doctor's office, but even so, sometimes modern medications don't work very well on the condition. So you may want to turn to home remedies for assistance. Once again, however, make sure that, however you treat your rheumatism with home remedies, the doctor knows about it so his medications won't conflict. While those used in home remedies don't sound very dangerous, they can sometimes nullify the effect of doctor-prescribed medications. If you want to make a tea for your condition, try alfalfa, allspice, and cranberry. You may also make apple tea and eat asparagus to counter the effects. Black currant helps, as do cayenne and celery.

Coriander and dandelion teas are home remedies, and horseradish, kidney beans and mother of thyme make fine medications. Oat, pansy, and poplar make poultices that you can put on the painful appendage. Red sage and rosemary, as well as rue, also can be used in poultices. You can make sarsaparilla and sassafras teas, and eat watercress. A poultice of white mustard and wild clover with willow makes a strong poultice. Wintergreen and witch grass also make fine poultices. Take cranberry juice when you have a flareup of rheumatism and parsley should be taken for its medicinal value. But plain old aspirin seems to work as well as anything. Aspirin can almost be a home remedy these days with the numbers of ailments it's used to cure. But for the teas and poultices, be sure to check with your doctor to see if they'll do any harm. Some, he'll say, may not even go well with aspirin, so listen to his advice.

Sinus

A great many people have sinus conditions, and very often have to go for weekly medical treatments to clear it out over a period of time. Except for leeks, which you can take as food, the rest of these remedies should be considered for poultices on your forehead and nose and cheeks. Blue flag and coltsfoot and eucalyptus make fine poultices for your condition. Also consider garlic you can eat as well as make into a poultice with goldenseal and ivy. Hyssop and mullein can also make a fine poultice. Just lay the poultice on your face and let the plants do their magic. Camphor can help if you rub it around your nostrils, and that granddaddy of all home remedies, Vicks Vaporub, is excellent when you have sinus problems.

Skin

If you have rough spots on your skin, then treat them with a poultice of elder, barberry, and birch, either separately or together. Black walnut and buck bean and buttercup as well as celandine and celery make fine poultices. The celery you can eat as well. If you have a rash, try chervil and chicory, but if it persists, ask your doctor what it may mean. The skin is a great prognosticator of troubles elsewhere in the body, so you always want to keep on top of what your skin is telling you. Common lettuce may be taken as a remedy, along with cucumber. English ivy makes a fine poultice, and so does English walnut. If you're not allergic to weeds, then you might try a poultice of goldenrod. And European vervain and primrose also may be used as poultices on small bumps and moles. Always be careful of moles, however, as any change in them might indicate a more serious skin problem. So really check your moles now and then to see if they're still the same.

Sleep

Remedies for sleeplessness are tricky when purchased at a drugstore by prescription. There are pills for sleep that are highly addictive, and getting out from under pill addiction is just terrible (I've known some people who have been through the withdrawal). So if you can take a home remedy that works but isn't addictive, then you're really ahead of the game. Chamomile is excellent as a tea to put you to sleep. Have a cup before lying down. Sage and clove are other remedies, and lavender and balm as poultices over your eyes are recommended. Try to stay away from drugs for inducing sleep, if you can, as they may make you feel lethargic in the morning. If you've taken them with alcohol, then they're dangerous. A cup of chamomile or clove tea is much superior as a sleep remedy than most of the other prescriptions that exist. Hot cocoa is another one from childhood that works, and a cup of hot milk just before lying down will also do the trick most of the time. If you're having insomnia because of worry, pull out your Bible and read soothing psalms or the words of the Apostles, and you should soon lose your anxiety and fall soundly asleep. But really try to stay away from medicines if you can as becoming a pill head is not desirable and is sometimes impossible to shake. I feel terribly sorry for Elizabeth Taylor who used painkillers for back problems and became addicted to them. She really had a struggle on her hands, and so can you if you get involved with prescription drugs for pain or sleep. Here's to chamomile and the other remedies.

They're just what the doctor ordered.

Smoking

To stop smoking, whether you're taking Nicorette gum or a home remedy (and there are just a few that I trust), there is really only one way to quit. That is cold turkey. A three-to-four-pack-a-day person, I told my internist about my addiction and he took a chest X-ray. After carefully studying it, he told me, "You don't have cancer yet." That was the beginning of the end of smoking for me. I felt I had a reprieve, a second chance to avoid lung cancer. And within a few months of that session with the doctor, I did quit. I had made a pact with myself that I would finish the carton of cigarettes that I had on hand, and then smoke no more. So with my last pack on my office desk, and a final cigarette in hand, I called in a few friends and told them to watch me smoke this last weed. They did and that was it. It's been over a year, a very hard long year, since I quit, but I know now I most probably won't die from lung cancer. For a home remedy to help ease the side effects of giving up smoking, try chamomile tea. Chamomile soothes and calms your nerves, and when you feel yourself craving a smoke, have a sip of the tea that you should keep on hand for this purpose. Peppermint is the other tea I would recommend for sipping to stop the craving. You will find, most probably, that when you give up smoking you develop a craving for sweets. Just ride the tide because the craving is very strong for sugar and you can't really successfully fight it. You can get it under some control, but the craving satisfied by cigarettes is left as a sore to be felt in the need for sugar. You're just going to have to put off your girlish figure or manly frame for the time being until the craving for sugar slowly starts to subside. You can try hypnotism, which I did, to help with the craving and it works to some degree. But expect it and you won't be in for nasty surprises—like a sudden size twelve figure where you used to be a nine or ten.

Sore Throat

You should make a gargle out of the herbs recommended for a sore throat, and you should take the gargle while it's still lukewarm. Black currant may be used as a gargle or a drink to soothe your throat. And comfrey can be used, but just as a gargle. Fenugreek makes a fine gargle and ginger tea is soothing for the condition. There really aren't any good over-the-counter remedies for a sore throat, as the ailment is a middle-point between healthy and sick. So home remedies hold just about as much hope of soothing a sore throat as do those remedies from a drug store. What I've noticed about the condition of city dwellers as opposed to those who live in the clean air of the countryside, is that urbanites more often get a sore throat, but before they know it, they've got bronchitis, even pneumonia. So I never take chances when I get a sore throat. I quickly take penicillin or some other antibiotic that's good for bronchitis, and kill the infection before it really becomes severe. I recommend that you keep antibiotics on hand (if you live in the city) and take them as soon as a sore throat comes on. You may wish to check a doctor if you do this to see if the herbs I've recommended for teas clash with the antibiotics he prescribes. Sage and savory also make good teas and are very soothing to your sore throat. Wintergreen makes a fine gargle, so you should make some and have it on hand.

Stomach

If you have a stomachache and know it came from eating too much, try one of the following remedies, like alfalfa and allspice made into a decoction to drink. You may just not be the sort of person who swears by Alka Seltzer (as I do) for a tummy condition, but prefers a home remedy, so go to it. Anise is another remedy. But if you have an ulcer or some other major stomach condition, I would take what the doctor ordered. These remedies are to soothe your condition, but, again, their interaction with modern drugs is pretty much an unknown quantity. Basil makes a nice tea, and of course, chamomile. Caraway and chicory and clove also make soothing teas as well as fennel. Garden thyme and garlic can be made into remedies, and ginger, too, although I would think that the ginger might be a bit too spicy for an already aggravated stomach. Hops and horehound are good stomach caretakers, and Iceland moss, too, if you can ever find any. Nutmeg is soothing, and so is papaya, which you may eat whole. Plantain and sage are good when you have a burning sensation. In the spring, collect wild strawberries because they're a wonderful remedy for stomach conditions. Boil the leaves and berries into a decoction for a tea, and you'll feel much better as a result of your remedy. You just can never be sure, though, if the remedy you've made will really work quickly enough for you, while you know that over-the-counter drugs work well. But if you want, try the home remedy method; you may be pleasantly surprised.

Sores

If you have strange sores, my advice is go to a dermatologist as they might mean that you have a fungal infection. I've spent time in the South Pacific and sores are common there that have to be treated medically. Psoriasis, for example, is very difficult to treat, and the treatment isn't all that successful. You might try a home remedy on that if you've got it. And the skin, especially in Washington, is subject to small dry spots that seem to have something to do either with the water or the air pollution. These particular sores are not dangerous, but they are irritating and itchy. These may be treated with home remedies, such as ointments to put on your sores. Use petroleum jelly to make the ointment and use goldenseal as the ingredient. You can also try comfrey, cabbage juice, and myrrh. Use with the vaseline, and keep the sore covered for a day or two with the ointment. Don't cover it with bandages if possible because the air needs to get at the sore.

Sprains

You'll want to baby your sprained ankle or hand and you'll need poultices like burdock and dock to spread on the surface of the sprain. Look for these unusual herbs in a shop selling nature foods and other items of the vegetarian and herbal use customers. Ginger is a remedy, too, as well as onion. Anything that eases a sprain will be good for you, and don't forget to fix some chamomile tea to help soothe the injury and keep your calm. You might try boneset as a poultice and hyssop. But whatever you use, make certain that you have an X-ray taken to verify a sprain and not a broken bone. The terrible pain associated with a sprain can make you think your limb is broken so always check to be sure it isn't.

Swelling

I've been noticing, as I get older, that I retain water more, causing a swelling of the ankles and, sometimes, fingers. A modern diuretic would be an over-the-counter or prescribed pill, but another way of dealing with swelling is with home remedies. Plantain may be eaten, and that's good for the condition. You also can make parsley tea, another antidote. Witch hazel rubbed on swelling helps and castor oil may do some good. Carrot is still another remedy for the condition. If you have swelling due to other reasons, you need to seek medical attention, but if it is just a case of water retention, then try the remedies. Naturally, if they don't work, ask your doctor about what he recommends for your condition. You don't want to suffer needlessly and do something silly like not looking after your health.

Tonics

Sometimes when you get home from work or after strenuous yard work, you need to sit still to change your energy. To add to the process, take a home remedy to perk you up while you're resting. Alfalfa has the tonic effect, and anise, basil, and peppermint all make fine teas for pick-me-ups. Carrot is, believe it or not, a tonic, so you may wish to take out your blender and make some carrot juice for yourself. Raspberry is also a tonic, and you can put that through a blender, too. Watercress is a pick-me-up, and you can eat that whole, or make sandwiches with it, but be careful of watercress, because you might be allergic to it as I am. I break out in hives when I eat fresh watercress, so I always have it cooked and then it doesn't have the same effect.

Tonsils

Tonsils are not to be fooled around with at any age. When the doctor says they must come out, then they must come out. After the tonsils are out, you'll likely want to soothe your throat. Ask your doctor's permission first, then go ahead with your home remedies. Make gargles of betony, goldenseal, and lemon, and you'll feel better. Peppermint is fine for tonsils, as are sage and tansy. Willow and witch hazel rubbed on your throat and chest will make you feel better. My younger brother had to have his tonsils out when he was twenty-one, and he was unable to talk for days. It's a much more serious operation as you get older, and in my generation, school kids were routinely having their tonsils out. I didn't have mine removed, but I've also had a history of throat problems. If you do have to have them taken out, treat your throat to ice cream (the traditional remedy after the operation) and teas. Naturally, chamomile, but parsley makes a nice tea. Stick with the gargles, however, especially in the early stages of recovery, and you'll soon be your old self again.

Toothache

Toothache, as far as I'm concerned, means one thing—root canal. I've had many root canals and they all began with a toothache. If you can't get to your dentist, take a home remedy until you can find out what's really wrong with your tooth. After all, it might just be sensitive to cold or heat, which sometimes happens out of the blue. Clove is a major remedy, and I'd get some tincture of clove and rub it on my tooth. Sassafras is a fine remedy for a toothache; try to apply it directly to your tooth. Take some chamomile tea, too, and you'll be fine till you make your dental appointment.

Urination

If you find you have trouble urinating, then you need to find out why. I recommend a doctor as always to see if it's a symptom for some other condition, but if it isn't, then a home remedy might do to speed up your bodily process. Asparagus will help speed up the process of urinating, as will black currant. I wish you all could have some of my mother's black currant jelly, which she served to go with meats and breads. Since none of us had urination problems, perhaps the currant jelly helped. Buttercup is another remedy, as well as carrot and celery. You can blend these ingredients and drink them as a juice, or make decoctions and turn them into teas. Chervil and chicory are other ingredients for the condition of slow urination. And dandelion tea (if you're not allergic to it) is a fine remedy for your condition, as are both horseradish and Indian corn. Kidney beans are wonderful antidotes to urination problems, as is licorice (the old fashioned kind of drops of pure licorice that my father used to use). The licorice drops Dad had were triangular in shape and pure black. They didn't taste awfully good so they were never meant to be eaten as candy. But Father used them as a digestive as he had terrible stomach upset, and it's interesting that licorice is also an antidote to urinary problems. Onion is also good for slow urination, as well as pansy and parsley. Make some teas of these ingredients and see if the condition doesn't relieve itself. Radish is another remedy for urinary tract problems, and so are willow and witch grass. You'll have to do some shopping around for these ingredients, but you might make yourself into an expert at recognizing herbs in the fields. Or better still, raise your own herbs at home.

Vaginal Douche

A great many female problems can be treated successfully with douching, so you might try your own remedy. It's important, however, to get a diagnosis as to what problem you have, for if it's a yeast infection, you need to get rid of it right away. A friend of mine with this infection didn't treat it properly and it has grown into a major problem with skin sores and what have you. And she's not allowed to eat any sugar because the yeast feeds on that as well as a variety of other foods. It's a nasty condition and extremely difficult to get rid of, so if you have a yeast infection, heed what the doctor tells you. If it's some simpler condition, then ask his permission to douche with homemade remedies. If he says yes, then try one made of barberry or birthroot, or black walnut. Fenugreek may be used as a douche, as can French rose and goldenseal. Hollyhock and Indian pipe are also good douching substances. We used to raise these on our land as I was growing up. It's interesting to know that Indian pipe is a useful douching ingredient as it's such a strange looking plant. Magnolia can be used by Southern women, and milfoil and myrrh are good for people living anywhere in the country. Pomegranate can be used by Westerners, and silvery lady's mantle can be used by everyone. White pond lily may be used as a douche, as can wintergreen. Witch hazel can be used but as with it and other douches, check your doctor before using any of them. He may wish you to use a douche's he's prescribed, so see if you can use your remedy instead of (or perhaps with) the one he recommends. After all, you don't want to slow down the healing process, so make sure that what you've got corresponds to a douching regime.

Varicose Veins

These unattractive lines on our legs as we get older can be treated by an operation, but for the most part, people don't have the time and money and just let their varicose veins stay. But if you don't have them removed, you can at least treat them with a home remedy poultice to make them feel and look better. Concoct a poultice of barberry and let it sit for ten or fifteen minutes on your veins. Hawthorn and horse chestnut are among the healing bushes and trees that can be used to fix a poultice. And sassafras is another remedy and smells so wonderful too. Shepherd's purse makes a fine poultice as do sticlewort and marjoram. Witch hazel may be the most soothing of all because you may buy it in a bottle and apply with cotton. It's very much like using alcohol as a home remedy. Particularly popular in the South for problems of the skin, witch hazel is a home remedy for all occasions. And if it isn't strong enough, then alcohol (of the rubbing variety) is used in its place. We use witch hazel all the time in our home and it's very good for minor skin irritations.

Warts

For a wart, you may want to rub it with the poultice and then wrap the poultice around it. You need to do this for a period of days to see if it works. I recommend Compound W which is an over-the-counter drug that does wonders on warts, but if you don't want to use it, then you might try a home remedy. Alder buckthorn is a fine poultice as are dandelion and fig tree. Garlic, leek, and lemon all are good remdies, and milkweed may be used, as well as mullein or spurge. Wild sage is another choice. If the wart doesn't disappear, then see a doctor or try Compound W.

There are still more substances that can be used as wart erradicators. Cayenne, apple juice, and cabbage should be eaten and drunk. And poultices made of chickweed and dandelion may be just what you need to remove a recalcitrant wart. To drink, try fig juice, and to eat, try leek, pineapple, and watercress. The watercress may be used as a poultice, too, as can the leek, but you wouldn't want to make a poultice of pineapple due to its thorny skin. Warts are an especially touchy subject with me now, as my body has acquired some and I'm going to a dermatologist to find out if I'm alright or if melanoma exists. My father developed lots of warts in old age, and it just might be that my system is taking after his, but I certainly want to know just what's going on because cancer is something I don't want to die of.

Worms

If you have a case of worms, it will show up in your feces. This kind of disease is not something you want to play around with so you must see a doctor about it. But, again, with his permission, you might try some herbal remedies to get rid of them. Aloe is recommended, and carrot juice or English walnut is a tea that may help, as well as garlic soup or juice made in a blender. Leek may be eaten or fixed as a tea, as can thyme. You may also eat onion and papaya (which, as far as I'm concerned is best as a tonic to keep your strength up), and pomegranate is recommended for this condition. Tansy and tarragon may work well with a worm condition, and wild plum can, too. Drink carrot juice and you might add cayenne pepper to the juice, and horseradish is recommended as well as lemon. You might try pumpkin as a worm antidote and make it into a tasty pie or into a soup.

II

Other Medicinal Herbs and Home Remedies

Agrimony

Agrimony is an herb for all seasons and does much for a variety of conditions. I recommend it particularly for gum problems (short of having a root canal) and sore throats (short of bronchitis) by using it as a gargle. It is also said to be very good at healing wounds, so you may wish to try it sometime on a bleeding scratch. I have tried agrimony as a mouthwash, and have found it helpful in keeping colds (which I get easily) at bay.

Aloe

Aloe is another all-around medication that I recommend for being especially helpful on burns and cuts. The way to use aloe is to keep a plant in the kitchen window. If you get burned or cut in the kitchen while preparing a meal, just snip a piece of aloe from the plant and rub it over the wound. Aloe helps the skin to heal. The gel is in the plant's leaves and is the miracle cure for burns and cuts. In the Caribbean, aloe grows wild on the hillsides and is such a big plant, but it may take an islander to point you in the right direction. As it is against the law to import the aloe from the Caribbean, the Food and Drug Administration will likely confiscate your plant if you bring it home with you from the islands. So try buying one in a plant store.

Angelica

This ancient remedy is good for indigestion, and indeed, in hot infusion, is good for colds. You want to have the roots on hand to make into a hot infusion, and always purchase angelica from someone who knows the plant well, as it is like several other poisonous ones and you might just pick one of them instead. I recommend always going to a knowledgeable herbalist, since as a child, I was admonished not to pick this herb or plant because of the poisonous properties. Many beautiful weeds, and herbs, and flowers are just not safe to have around. So mother taught me a healthy respect for the flora in our area. I was allowed, however, to pick wild raspberries that grew on our property, and they were delicious!

Anise

I've mentioned anise before, but I want to emphasize that it's especially good for stomach pain. If you have gas pains, or pains that you know are just temporary, then take some anise tea and you should feel better right away. Over-the-counter drugs are pretty well advanced to treat stomach pains that aren't serious, so your use of anise is strictly a matter of your taste and interest in home remedies. If you don't live near a drugstore, then anise may be just what you need because it's what you probably can find at hand.

Arnica

This is the famous wolf's bane used to counter the condition of lycanthropy in werewolf lore. Arnica is a dangerous herb that you can't use yourself as it can cause rash in some people. It's used for bruises, and depending on their size, you might be better off just letting them heal themselves. You'd need to buy arnica in a health food store or place where homeopathic remedies are sold, and realize it's dangerous when improperly used.

Asparagus

I've also recommended the use of asparagus as a medication, and I will again. It's especially good for urinary tract problems. You need not do anything fancy with the asparagus, just prepare it to eat, and you'll be eating a fine remedy for your interior organs. The stems and tip and even the root of this plant are good.

Barberry

This herb is used as a digestive tonic, and is good for the liver and gallbladder as well. While it should not be used if you're pregnant, it is good (with the permission of your doctor, of course) if you're being treated for liver or gallbladder problems. If he isn't sure what effect your Western medication has on barberry, then don't take it as the side effects may be dangerous. You use the bark and fruit to make your tonic, and be sure that you don't overdose yourself with it. Take no more than two cups of tea a day made from barberry as it is strong medication.

Bayberry

My earliest memory of bayberry were the candles made of it that Mother bought on Cape Cod and always used on the mantelpiece at Christmas. On Christmas Day, she would light them, and they would scent the room where we had our tree and opened or gifts and listened to the Brandenburg Concertos on the record player. I don't think Dad missed filming Christmas Day festivities during our entire childhood. Aside from making candles of it, bayberry is also useful medicinally as an astringent. One of its uses is as a douche, and a decoction may be used to treat colds. It makes a fine gargle and a poultice of the plant helps with cuts and sores. You don't want to use it for a long period of time because it can become toxic, but as a gargle for sore throats and a poultice for cuts, it's especially recommended.

Wood Betony

This is a fine remedy for head colds. You need to make a powder of the flowers and, taking it like snuff, put it up your nostrils and soon the betony will break up your head cold. You may also use betony as a poultice for bruises, wrapping the bruises with the leaves.

Blue Cohosh

One of the properties of this medication is that it's good for cramps women sometimes experience with their periods. The root is the part that you will be interested in, and you can prepare it as a decoction. Be careful not to get near the seeds, as they're poisonous. American Indians used this herb, and you should partake of the tea sparingly as, in the old days, it was used for childbirth. It's strong medication and should never be taken if you're pregnant.

Boneset

This is the herb to use for the flu or a cold that may resemble the flu in intensity. You must use it as a hot infusion to start the sweat that breaks the fever. There are a number of fine remedies for colds and flus, but boneset is a traditional Indian remedy which they gave to the settlers who passed it on through the generations. If you have arthritis or rheumatism, you may wish to try boneset as a poultice to stop the pain. It's sometimes used that way, but its reputation as a flu antidote is strongest.

Borage

Here's another herb I haven't mentioned so far. It's good for depression, a condition you don't want to fool around with. You have to be aware of what kind of depression you have—the sort that lasts for a day or two, or that hangs on for months and makes you think of suicide? If you have a mild, short-term depression, then you can take borage for it. But if you have the dangerous long-term kind, you'd best take what a psychiatrist recommends (Elavil or some other new antidepressant). Once you're on medication for one of the mental illnesses that may beset us at any time in our lives, then you're off on a great dialogue with others who take medications and with your doctor. The reaction to medications is different with each individual. Use the leaves to make a tea, and the flowers may also be used for this purpose. Pray that the depression lifts, because it's among the deadliest of all mental illnesses.

Brazil Wood

Brazil wood should be purchased in an herbal shop, especially one dealing in Central and South American remedies. It's very good for anxiety and you must ask your herb doctor how he feels about your taking it. I myself have discovered Brazil wood to be a fine remedy for light cases of anxiety. If there is too much, such as I found out myself, then you may need a so-called modern miracle drug to take away the symptoms. That's what I've done and I feel a thousand percent better for having found the medication. Brazil wood just wasn't strong enough for me, but with your doctor's knowledge, try it for yourself if you're not overwhelmed with anxiety.

Broom

You don't want to try taking this without a doctor's advice as it is used to regulate the heart. It is also used as a diuretic, but since it's a volatile plant and is qualified by the FDA as unsafe, you won't want to take this without a herbalist's knowledge. But, as you can see, it is powerful and you can discuss with your doctor and herbalist its use for you if you have a heart condition.

Burdock

This plant, all of it, may be used as a diuretic, or as a tonic to purify the blood. It can be used in cooking, but it's effective for its laxative effect. This is one of those herbs that's good for a great many disorders. Among them is cystitis, but I don't think I'd try to treat that condition with a home remedy. I'd see my doctor for that. But burdock is good for a wide variety of disorders, and as a diuretic, it would be helpful for high blood pressure. However, you'd need to see a doctor for that because it would depend on what medication he prescribes.

Camphor

Camphor is one of my favorite remedies as it was given to me as a child by my grandmother if I had a cold. She rubbed it on my chest and back, and since it's already a treatment for rheumatism, I got the benefit of a rubbing for that. Grandmother always carried a small camphor container in her purse, and, as women did in those days, would sniff it if feeling faint. The caution is not to take too many sniffs of the camphor because of its powerful effects. But the camphor oil is definitely recommended for rheumatic joints. Rub the oil on the affected joint and the pain should begin to clear up quickly.

Centaury

A traditional remedy for gout or rheumatism, centaury flowers are what make the medication. Centaury also can be used to treat heartburn—it's used in some alcoholic drinks as a bitter flavor and tonic effect—and for reducing fever. It's still used in the Middle East for treating high blood pressure, and is thought to work well on depression. I've used it as a remedy for heartburn and wound up with my Alka Seltzer. After going to all the trouble to make a gargle and then find that Alka Seltzer works just as well is a disappointment that a great many herbalists face. You don't want to become so dedicated to herbal remedies that you overlook the drugstore for appropriate medications. Since quantities are not always known for taking of these remedies, it's wise, when there's an unknown, to take no more than two cups of herbal tea a day. Always abide by any instructions that point to an herb having side effects like sores around the mouth, etc. Herbs can be treated as powerful medications, and their use should be preceded by good medical advice. If you're really going to turn to herbal remedies for everything, then you need to study the subject and get to know a homeopathic doctor who can advise you.

Chamomile

Here is *the* all-around home remedy herbal tea to take. It does exactly the same things as wild lettuce, but it's better known and more reliable. If you have insomnia, it will put you gently to sleep. If you have anxiety or nervous stomach, it will soothe you and calm your nerves. I recommend chamomile for anything at all to do with nerves. And if you count sheep into the thousands and are still awake, then get out of bed and brew some chamomile tea. Try this tea before going to the medicine chest for an over-the-counter or prescribed sleeping medication. You will have the same result without taking on the risks of some of the modern medications. They're also not good to have around the house if you have children. But chamomile is a safe, sound remedy if you need it.

Wild Cherry

It's interesting to note, since people eat wild cherry just off the tree, that its leaves and cherry pits are poisonous. Don't eat them. But the bark of the tree bought prepared is the perfect antidote to a prolonged cough. An acquaintance of mine has a persistent cough from draining sinuses, aggravated by his continual smoking. He said, ''I don't know what's causing this cough,'' because he's denying that it's the cigarettes as he doesn't want to give them up. If he ever takes the wild cherry remedy, he would find it at least as good as cough drops, and longer lasting in effect

Chickweed

This plant is widely used as a poultice for skin problems. If you have a rash or a boil, use the poultice as recommended, but not before you check with your doctor. It might just be a skin condition that responds well to home remedies, but you want to make certain of that. If you have a boil or some other problem that seems to be on the serious side, don't use your home remedy first. Consult your doctor first. That's what I'd recently done with a boil I got on the bridge of my nose, suddenly overnight. My doctor told me to give it two weeks and it should be healed. Since he didn't say I couldn't use a remedy on it, I'd been using chickweed. It took a week instead of two for the boil or whatever it was to go down, and now I'm all right again. So I saw my doctor first, and since he didn't recommend any medical treatment for it, I felt I could use my home remedy on it and see if it went away faster. It did and I'm pleased.

Chicory

Chicory is one of those herbs that's good as a digestion tonic. It's also useful for a variety of other ailments (as discussed in the first section) but it's especially good for anemia and rheumatism. As an additive to coffee, or a substitute, chicory is well-known, especially in the South. So it has stimulative powers along with its bitter taste. The root is the part of the plant that is used as a coffee additive or substitute, and it is also good for the gout as it cleanses the blood of uric acid. I personally find chicory too bitter for my tastes, but if someone has rheumatism or gout or needs to cleanse the blood with a strong tonic, I recommend chicory to accomplish the job. Don't get involved with too much of it, though, as it's a strong root and the medication it makes is very powerful.

Chilies

I have a friend who takes herbal remedies and she always has chilies at least once a day. She says there's very little incidence of heart attack in Mexico and South America because of the chilies they eat all the time. In fact, chilies are a stimulant to the heart, and cayenne, which is one of the chilies, is very powerful indeed. Asians also use lots of chilies and remain healthy—or used to before they discovered cigarettes and alcohol and other Western drugs. But you must be aware that the overuse of chilies is bad for the liver and can cause kidney disorders, so you must be very careful about the dosage. Look for cayenne chilies in their pods, and you'll have a handy medication to treat a healthy heart. There are so many miracles about saving heart attack patients these days in modern hospitals, that it seems the only use for chilies is as a preventive medicine. Try to get further opinions on the efficacy of chilies as a heart remedy and stimulant before taking them, and don't forget, too many are not good for you.

I want to also mention that chilies are very good for late menstruation. Don't take too many of them at any one time because they can be very hard on your insides. But if your menstruation is off, then it's time to break out a chili and eat one a day till your period is back on track. You don't want to sit there eating chilies if, by any chance, you're pregnant, so consult your doctor if you suddenly feel that this might be the early stages of pregnancy that you're experiencing.

Cinnamon

The dried herb of cinnamon is what you want both for cooking and for medical remedies. It's especially good for colds and diarrhea. You may chew on the bark or let it steep into a tea, and it will do you some good. I can't imagine drinking a hot toddy without a stick of cinnamon to ease the annoyance of a runny nose. You might try using it if you're having trouble with menstrual cramps. As a drink to soothe you after a long day at work, I recommend making iced tea and adding several cinnamon sticks to the mixture. It's very soothing and a little sedative, if used properly.

Cinnamon is good for a variety of upper respiratory ailments, but it's best for a persistent cough, brought on by smoking or by a cold. Make a tea of the cinnamon bark and, if you're not an alcoholic, add some spirits. It's a very soothing remedy for your complaint.

Cleavers

This herb is good (use its above-ground leaves and stems) for skin diseases such as eczema and psoriasis. That is, it's good when the condition is not complicated by being a symptom of something else. If you have eczema, you need to consult a doctor. Take the remedy he prescribes, but also tell him about cleavers and that you want to use it. If you ask an herbal doctor, he may give you the go-ahead.

Clove

I've recommended clove for other complaints but it's especially good as an oil to treat teeth. I've had oil of clove many times put on my teeth before the filling was put in, because ot is antiseptic properties. It's used in the Middle East as a breath freshener; I once knew a fellow from Morocco who always carried a small vial of cloves around to chew. It's used, of course, extensively in cooking, and in such goodies as a potpourri apple which we used to make in school when I was a child. The apple was stuck full of cloves, then given to your mother for her stocking drawer as a Christmas present.

Comfrey

This plant may be used as a poultice for taking care of burns, bruises, or sprained ankles, or even some fractures. So you won't get in the way of modern medicine and its splints and the like, ask your doctor if you can use comfrey on whatever ails you. With his permission, go ahead and make poultices. The fresh leaves of this plant are also used to make teas for your digestive tract. It seems that it's a very good medication for a burning sensation in the stomach. Of course, with this burning, you should find out what's wrong with you. It could be an ulcer, and there are modern methods of treating them now that have taken this common complaint to near extinction. If you're certain you don't have an ulcer, but maybe just are a little gassy, then go ahead and drink comfrey tea.

Coriander

The coriander, when fried and eaten, is good for an earache. You may have an ear infection with the ache so you need to seek medical advice about what's wrong with you. But for the meantime, coriander will help. I keep thinking that the people who will be using these remedies live in the country and are already knowledgeable about what plants are good and can identify those needed for medication. But one really needs to be an expert to feel safe in doing that. A friend of mine who grew up in the country and was visiting me, saw some poke salad growing in the backyard of my city apartment some years ago. He said, "Oh, poke salad. I'll just pick that and cook it and we'll have it as greens with our dinner." Not knowing a thing about it, I ate what he cooked and it was very good. Some years later, while reading about herbs, there was poke salad with a great big warning about how poisonous it was if not fixed properly. I was shaken a bit, but my country friend knew how to fix it. I'm careful now and recommend that you seek medical advice before treating yourself with one of the herbs like coriander that may turn out to be very bad for you if taken in the wrong dosage or if you have an allergy. Before taking these herb concoctions internally, have an herbal doctor tell you about the herbs you're planning to use as remedies. Then you'd have a second opinion on what's good for you, how to prepare it, and how much to take.

Indian Corn

I've recommended this herb for a number of conditions, and here again it is used for urinary infections. The silk that comes with corn can be made into a diuretic, and is good for urinary tract infections. It may also be used to lower blood pressure, though that's a condition that requires appropriate medical attention. As a food, we all know that corn is delicious and full of nutrition. As a remedy, it's up there with the other herbs that do wonders, and you don't have to worry about ingesting the corn as it's not poisonous. As long as you're not allergic to it, this is a fine plant to use as diuretic, and as an aid to curing urinary infection.

Corn Tassel

To clean out the kidneys, corn tassel tea is an excellent remedy. You just boil the corn tassel and let it sit for a while, then take a taste of the tea. Don't take more than two or three teas on a given day, and let them cool before drinking. Your kidneys will benefit from the washing they get with the tea. I don't recommend seven or eight cups in a day as some herbalists do for cleansing teas, as I just don't think it's safe. Two teas should be enough with which to treat yourself. If you take more than that in a day, talk to your herb doctor about proper amounts. I firmly believe that with most of the medications in this book, you need to have an herb doctor nearby to recommend amounts to be taken and also the interaction between modern medicine and herbal remedies. If you're taking something from a physician, you should know as soon as you can if your teas are interfering with the medication. Knowing the dangers is a new area for medical doctors, so you'd best find one who knows herbs and consult him.

Cowslip

Cowslip used to grow in the fields near my childhood home, and I used to smell their fragrance. Today, I find that they're medicinally helpful to nerves. Just fix a tea, and soothe your nerves with the flowers which you used to make the tea. The root is good for arthritis, but I'd ask the advice of an herbal doctor before preparing it for internal use. The plant offers a range of home remedy cures and is an all-around remedy.

American Cranesbill

This plant is used to stop diarrhea and bleeding. If you use the powdered root to stop bleeding, you will be exercising one of its uses. And if you take it as a gargle, it's good for sore throats. For diarrhea, you might try a decoction. Again, it's a toss-up whether to use one of the over-the-counter medications for diarrhea instead of going to the trouble of fixing American cranesbill. I can understand having the powder around to stop bleeding if you cut yourself with a kitchen knife. But as a gargle, I'm not sure. If the gargle works and all you had was a sore throat instead of a complicated upper respiratory infection, then all to the good. But these days with pollution causing combinations of diseases that seldom were seen, you have to take a more modern view of medications and realize that not all remedies are going to work.

Dandelion

With this particular plant, you need to be very sure that you're not allergic to it before using it. It's a wonderful diuretic when used as a tea, and the root makes a laxative if you're constipated. But the widely-used reason for taking dandelion tea is that it's a wonderful tonic for purifying the blood, and helping the liver and other organs to rid themselves of poisons that build up in the body. If you rub the dandelion sap on a wart, the lore is that the wart will be removed. I would guess you'd do better with Compound W, but you certainly are welcome to try the dandelion sap as a wart remover. If you're positive you're not allergic to dandelion, then you may wish to use the leaves in salads as greens cooked as you would spinach. There are lots of ways dandelions may be used either as a home remedy or as a food.

Elder

I've mentioned elderberry tea as a remedy for colds, but it's also good for flus (if you get your doctor's permission to drink the tea while using medications). The flowers are used and a tea may be made from them. Elderberry is used in some foods as flavoring, so it's definitely safe to drink. If you've got a mild infection in your eye, you can use the elderberry as an eyewash. Again, if modern day eyewashes are better, then stick with them. I don't really recommend home remedies when, very often, modern medicine has produced a much better antidote. But very often home remedies do the job better than any other medication, and many of the recipes in the first section are geared to conditions for which modern medicine just hasn't really found a cure. But if you are looking for a good pick-me-up and tonic, try making some elderberry tea.

Elderberry tea is one that often appears in literature. Little old ladies in a number of books in the early twentieth century would take elderberry tea together. Why, I don't know, given that the tea is used for abdominal pain. And as with all remedies for stomach pain, I recommend that you find out what's wrong with you from a physician. There are many conditions that drinking elderberry tea won't help, and you need to know if you have one of these. If you don't, and you have simple indigestion, then elderberry tea is a wonderful remedy to take, and I recommend it highly. It's also used as a treatment for measles and fever, but don't take more than two cups of the tea per day without a doctor's permission. He may have other remedies in mind for breaking a high fever.

Eucalyptus

This herbal plant is a favorite with panda bears as food, and medicinally, it's good for colds. The oil is used externally as an inhaler, and can be diluted to make a rubbing oil for the chest. The caution with eucalyptus is not to take it internally as it can be poisonous for humans.

Eyebright

This remedy is good for itchy eyes and hayfever. You must never put anything in your eyes without consulting a physician, so try your herb doctor on this one before using eyebright. It's also good for colds when your sinuses are full, and can be used as a gargle for a sore throat. There are so many wonderful unguents for the eyes when they're inflamed or have other conditions that it doesn't seem logical to treat them with eyebright. But, of course, if you are living in the wilderness and don't have easy access to a doctor, the thing to do is carefully use as a compress over your eyes and see if they feel better when you take it off. If so, use eyebright again later on, probably in the evening if you've used it in the morning. You can make an infusion to treat hayfever and other sneezing conditions, but you mustn't overlook Benedryl which may be bought over-the-counter. Many symptoms of allergy can be treated with Benedryl.

Fennel

Fennel is another all-around plant that's useful for a variety of conditions as a home remedy. It's very good for indigestion, and if you are off the use of Pepto Bismol or Alka Seltzer, this is for you. The seeds and the root both are good for digestive ailments and also may be helpful if you have kidney stones. I don't use fennel myself (although I've tried it) and I continue to recommend over-the-counter products for indigestion. But purists, I know, will want to try fennel, and it does its job reasonably well.

Fenugreek

This herb, as one of its remedial uses, is an aphrodisiac and also good during menopause to assuage the perspiration and combat menopausal depression. The seeds are the part to make into a tea. It's advised not to use fenugreek during pregnancy, so you need to be under the care of an herbal doctor before taking such strong medicine. It can also be used as a poultice if you have a boil that needs medication to break or draw up. I've recommended it as an aphrodisiac tea to a friend who now swears by it saying that her husband is much more loving after a cup of it.

Feverfew

This remedy is a sound one and has been tested by modern doctors. It's associated with being a fine cure for migraine headaches as well as an antidote to depression. The part of the plant that should be used to treat your illness is the leaf, and you can brew a fine tea with the leaves as long as you don't drink it more than twice a day. A warning about this herb: It can give you sores around your mouth, so be sure to stop using it if any of these should appear. If you do suffer from migraine, give feverfew a try. As long as nothing else works, you might as well see if this herb is the magic answer to your pain.

Flax

Flax oil and seeds have been used since the beginning of time to treat constipation and as a burn poultice. Another name for flax is linseed oil and this is used in paint and varnish. But flax as a poultice is highly recommended, and when it's in combination with slippery elm, it is very effective indeed. If you want to use it as a laxative, be sure to buy the right kind of flax oil that is suitable for consumption. A large dose of linseed can be very dangerous, and the age of the seeds has something to do with its poisoning capabilities. So buy it from an herbal outfit, and take it only in moderation.

Flour

If you toast flour, those of Spanish background say, you have a fine poultice for burns. Just wrap the flour around the burn. If you are without any other ointments or unguents in the house when a simple burn occurs, then try the toasted flour remedy. But if the burn is a bad one, see a physician. I

keep a little toasted flour in my kitchen in case I pick up a hot
pan or lid and accidentally give myself a little burn. But anything beyond that needs more important treatment.

Garlic

Now here is the classic of all remedies. It is used in witchcraft and medically, and you would always do well to have it
in your healing arsenal. Among its attributes are that it's good
for high blood pressure. I recommend that you take the medication the doctor gives you for high blood pressure, but ask
an herbal doctor if you can also take garlic as a blood pressure
reducer. He may say no, or not too high a dosage, but if it
comes down to a choice between medications, choose what
your doctor prescribes. Garlic is an all-around medication that
is also good for colds and as a digestive aid. Again, ask your
doctor what he thinks about your self-remedy. There is
research being done to see if garlic is a remedy for cancer, so
you already know that it's powerful medicine. The cloves are
the part of the garlic that you eat, and you can put them in
food if you don't like the strong garlic taste alone.

Balm of Gilead

The leaf buds of the balm of Gilead are the portion of the
plant to use to make a gargle. This remedy can be used with
sore throats to great effect, and is most useful the minute your
soreness comes on. You may be able to stop the infection causing it if you take the gargle at the first sign of the condition. It
has been my experience, after living in New York and
Washington for long periods of my life, that the minute you
get a sore throat in these cities, you invariably expect a case of
bronchitis to follow. So getting rid of a sore throat right away
is essential to continued good health. Once again, if you take
penicillin as your immediate antidote to sore throat followed
by bronchitis, then check with your doctor to see if balm of
Gilead is something you can use as a countermeasure, too. I
would think that in less polluted areas of the country where a
sore throat means you're going to get the common cold, then

you wouldn't have to worry so much about taking antibiotics right away. And you then could rely on balm of Gilead alone to ease your throat pain.

Oriental Ginseng

Ginseng, to the Oriental, is like chamomile tea to the Westerner, used as a tonic for weakness as well as its traditional use as an aphrodisiac. It's used for just about everything that can go wrong with you, and the effect is soothing and good for the nerves. Older people in the South seem troubled by nerves from time to time, and instead of seeing a psychiatrist, their doctors prescribed pills. On their own, they use remedies learned from their parents. Chamomile tea or ginseng is what they sip for their nerves. One interesting item about ginseng is that it's difficult to buy a good grade of it in the West. It is usually the weaker variety that is sold. So if you can do some research and get ginseng stock to raise yourself, you'd be much better off. You don't want to use ginseng when you've got a cold as it may make the cold worse. Its use is as a tonic, or aphrodisiac. And when you're searching for ginseng to grow, be sure you have the Chinese variety and not the much weaker American kind.

Golden Seal

Golden seal is good for the digestive system, and is used by herbal doctors to treat ulcers and other conditions. A mouthwash made of the golden seal is good for tender gums, and, as a gargle, for sore throats. You must be cautious with this remedy and don't use it if you're pregnant. It can have adverse affects.

Heather

This plant is usually used to treat asthma, and again, I'd be pretty certain that my physician knew I was taking heather before going off and doing it on my own. You might be allergic to the plant and be worse off than you were before. One of its properties is to clear up hayfever so it's not too likely that it will cause an allergy, but you should make certain that it doesn't in you. A warning about the herb: a large dose may cause nausea and vomiting. And heather is of a family of herbs and plants that are poisonous to people, so you should be careful with it in all respects.

Hops

Hops are a remedy I used a lot in the first section of this book. To elucidate further, they can be used for nervous tension which we all sometimes get, and for insomnia. They have many other herbal uses. You need to use the flowers to make your potion for sleeping and tension, and I've recommended hops as an antidote to Crohn's disease. Hops, of course, are used in the making of beer. They're also recommended for keeping ulcers from forming but if you drink too much beer, you may be certain that the hops will imitate the condition. So be careful about the quantity of hops you use if you feel an ulcer may be developing.

Horseradish

I've recommended horseradish for various conditions in the first section of this book and I'd like to add that it's good for the digestive tract. It happens to be good for gout, and is often used as a poultice for arthritis. There is a danger with horseradish, however, as too much of it can make blisters rise on the skin. You never want to use horseradish and drugs given to you for the thyroid condition. They don't mix and can be dangerous. If you want to stimulate your digestion, then make a decoction of horseradish and your listless stomach will perk right up. The horseradish root is the part of the plant that you use to make your remedies.

Hyssop

The medical uses for hyssop are for anything to do with the upper respiratory system such as a bad cold. This plant should be used with the supervision of a doctor because small doses can be harmful. There really is no cure for the common cold yet, so if you want to try hyssop, go right ahead. It's a very ancient remedy, used in Greece, and still going strong, though it's used carefully. It can also be used as a poultice for burns or bad bruises, and you might wish to keep hyssop around for these eventualities.

Iceland Moss

I haven't recommended this so far as it is rather an esoteric herb. You need to try a really well-stocked herb collection to find this lichen-like plant. But there are so many medicines that can treat asthma that it seems silly to go to all the trouble of getting this herbal remedy when medication is available. However, if you're an herbal diehard, then you'll want to have Iceland Moss on hand if you have asthma or plan to treat someone who does. If you're treating others, though, you definitely need the guidance of an herbal doctor.

Wild Indigo

If you have sores on your body as the side effect of certain conditions, such as candida albacans, you'll need to spread wild indigo on them to help them heal. You don't want to take too much of this herb internally as it has the effect of sometimes causing violent diarrhea, but if you have arthritis, you might try a poultice of wild indigo to soothe the affected parts. Of course, you wouldn't want to treat yourself with wild indigo unless the herb doctor agrees. My friend with the candida albacans had such a severe case of it that no herbal remedies worked and she eventually took doctor-prescribed medicine. It seems better, but not much. The sores were terrible, and cortizone cream didn't work well on them, so she used wild indigo to treat them with some effect. I haven't heard her complain lately about the sores she got from this condition, so I assume the wild indigo did well by her.

Irish Moss

If you buy some Irish moss, put it in water and watch it blossom into a gummy mass. Then you make a decoction of it and it becomes a gel which you can then use to treat ulcers. There are some wonder drugs that all but heal ulcers today, so using Irish moss is no longer necessary. But you may wish to eat it anyway as it is a fine food and makes you feel healthy.

Juniper

I've recommended juniper, and again, it's a fine remedy for gout and rheumatism. It's also useful in treating urithritis and for flatulence. If you chew the berries instead of making a decoction of them, they are said to relieve sore gums. But if you're going to use juniper, be aware that it's dangerous and should only be used internally under a doctor's supervision. The oil in the berries is potent and can affect someone with kidney disease or during pregnancy. Only a qualified herbalist doctor should treat you as the oil can turn out to be quite dangerous.

Lady's Slipper

These adorable flowers which I loved so much in childhood can be used to rid yourself of nervous tensions and headaches. This plant, however, has been used so much that it's now an endangered species. So if you're an environmentalist as well as an herbalist, you will not want to use lady's slipper. There are so many other remedies for nervous conditions without resorting to this plant, that I recommend you don't use it.

Lavender

Although you can't take lavender without close medical supervision, you can use it for burns and stings and not have to worry about taking it internally. Its aroma is also well known by daughters who remember their grandmother's sachets. My grandmother had a lavender sachet and she made me one, which I treasured for years. Lavender also can be used in an amulet for healing. I'd say keep it around to make into a poultice for burns or bee stings, and avoid turning it into a potion. I don't like to recommend any herb which is dangerous, and lavender is one of those which need supervision. There are just better herbs around for the same complaint that aren't just as dangerous to take internally. One other area where lavender may be used without getting into too much difficulty is as a douche. Some of its properties are good at killing infection, so it works as well as a douche as it does on a burn or sting.

Lemon Balm

Lemon balm is recommended for colds and flu. Fresh leaves of the lemon make an infusion which brings on sweating and is, therefore, good as a remedy for the flu. Since the plant has a sedative effect, it's also an old-time remedy for depression. No warnings come with lemon balm, but you certainly would want to know about side effects from your herb doctor if you're taking strong medication for depression. And if your doctor treats the flu with medication, you had better ask him about the effect of lemon balm with the substances prescribed. If you have sores around your mouth from a cold, the lemon balm is good for those too. It's quite a versatile medication, and one I favor. If someone tells me they've had a depressing day, I treat them with lemon balm to make them feel more like their better selves.

Licorice

I can attest to the worthiness of licorice for heartburn and ulcers. As I've mentioned before, my father took licorice for his bad stomach, and it really worked well. It lowers the acid in the stomach so that heartburn and ulcers aren't aggravated. There is only one warning with the herb: do not use it over a period when you have high blood pressure. It's also recommended that you not use licorice if you're pregnant or have problems with your kidney. It's hard to want to take licorice over a period of time in any event because it has a bitter flavor and is not altogether pleasant to imbibe. You may want to substitute licorice candies that are less bitter than the actual plant. I can't see that the candies are any less good for you than the original plant, and they certainly taste a lot better.

Lily-of-the-Valley

You cannot use this plant as a medicine as it has been restricted as poisonous by the FDA. But you'll be interested to know that there is research being done to see if the lily is a remedy for heart disease. It's just a shame that such a beautiful and potentially useful plant is also poisonous, but that sometimes happens. I wanted to tell you about the lily because you might have heard from other sources that it's okay to eat it. Actually, it's dangerous, so regard this passage as a warning against taking lily-of-the-valley as a remedy.

Limberbush

Those of Spanish descent in the Southwest and Mexico discuss a condition called weak blood. This is probably anemia and you need to take iron to adjust the blood to normal. But if you want to try your own remedy for weak blood, then take some limberbush tea. You'll have to go to the herb shop to find this one, and of course, that's half the enjoyment. Collecting exotic herbs and knowing what they're used for is a lot of fun when talking among friends about what's new and interesting herb-wise.

Lime Tree

Lime can be used for a variety of remedies if you use the flowers and inner bark. If you make an infusion of the lime leaves, you have an excellent remedy for colds. And lime-flower tea is an old remedy for hyperactivity. If you're just one of those people always on the go, be it shopping or at work, and you seek a soothing tea at the end of the day so you can get to sleep, then limeflower tea is what you need. The tree's inner bark is used to treat such important conditions as kidney stones, and I don't recommend it for such illnesses without the advice of a doctor who also knows herbs. If you've got kidney stones, there are modern ways to rid the body of them and they should be taken into consideration. Don't try to treat yourself with lime bark, but let the experts handle this one.

Mallow

Hispanics also use mallow as an enema if one has a fever. If the fever comes with a cold, then a mallow enema should be just the remedy. But if there is an unknown cause for the fever, then it's necessary to be diagnosed correctly. I just wouldn't treat a fever without knowing what was wrong with me. Fevers are usually symptoms of some serious diseases, and you'd want to be certain you weren't treating a condition with an herb that might not be right for it. But as an enema, mallow is a good remedy so go ahead and try it.

Marigold

I haven't talked about marigold, but it's a wonder antiseptic for burns and is a first-aid remedy as well. Use the flowers pressed against the burn to help heal it. As always, take care and don't be foolish. Modern medicine does wonders with burns, so if you've got a bad one, don't take matters into your own hands. Go to the emergency room of a hospital for treatment. But if you burn yourself on your iron or suffer a little burn from your stove, then you can try marigold poultices to make it feel and heal better.

Meadowsweet

This herb is good for diarrhea and for fevers. You use the flowers and leaves, and make them into a tea. There are no dangerous side effects that herbalists are aware of, and they tout it for many ailments, but I recommend it especially for diarrhea which is in a non-recurring form and not a symptom of something more serious. As for fevers, if your herbal doctor says it's okay to use it for them, go ahead. But fevers are usually a symptom of something else so you need to find out the cause of it before going about treating it.

Desert Milkweed

If you've been having trouble with your kidneys and want a tonic that will clean them out, then use desert milkweed as a tea and rest contented. You would have to get the milkweed from an herbal store, and, of course, check with your doctor before taking any. If you rely on an herbal doctor, as you should if you're taking herbs as remedies, he may suggest a substitute for the desert milkweed if it's hard to get near you.

Mistletoe

I mention mistletoe as it is the bearer of highly poisonous berries and should not be used internally unless prescribed by an herbal doctor for lowering blood pressure. American mistletoe is simply unsafe to use, and only a doctor would use it under severe circumstances. So your best bet with mistletoe is to stay away from it as a remedy.

Mountain Grape

This is a fine tonic if, like blue cohosh, you don't take it during pregnancy. It is used as a blood purifier, and if you're a vegetarian, you might be especially interested in this herb. But everyone needs to purify their blood sometime in their lives, and mountain grape is a good herb to take for this.

Mugwort

Like wormwood, this herb can cause a miscarriage and should be used only with professional supervision. It cannot be used during pregnancy, but at other times, it's good for regulating menstruation. It shouldn't be used for too long a time, and it's strong enough to start menstruation if it's stopped. Now this is a very fine capability (restarting a stopped period) except for one thing. Oftentimes an interrupted period indicates that something is wrong with the reproductive system. Therefore, you should consult a doctor to find out what's wrong with you rather than self-diagnose and take mugwort. If you've got homeopathic medical advice, this herb may be prescribed, but I certainly wouldn't take it without a medical doctor's knowledge.

Mullein

Mullein is one of the all-around remedies that herbal doctors rely on. It not only is good for respiratory complaints, but is a diuretic and can be used on rheumatoid joints. As a tea, it's soporific and makes you feel comfortable after sipping some. Take as a gargle to relieve coughs and other respiratory disorders. There are no major warnings about mullein, but you should always try a small dosage to see how it affects you, or, better yet, ask your herb doctor what dosage is correct for your condition.

Black Mustard

The seeds and leaves are the parts to use from this plant. A word of warning at the outset: Don't use much of this as it can cause your skin to blister. It's definitely not to be taken if you're using thyroid medication. Mustard is good for coughs and for indigestion, but I must say I prefer my old standby, Alka Seltzer, if my stomach is upset. If you don't use the over-the-counter digestive medications, then you might try a tea from the leaves to see if that helps. Use the seeds to make a poultice if you have a bad cough, and place the poultice on your chest for the best effect. You can also use mustard to stimulate circulation by using it in foot baths. It's just an all-around good herb, except that it must be used wisely and carefully because of its side effects. Take care when using this one!

Myrrh

Myrrh is a romantic herb due to the legend of its being carried as a gift by the Wise Men looking for baby Jesus. In modern times, myrrh is used for everything from sore throats to athlete's foot. The resin is the part of the herb that you can use, and it may be made into a gargle. In ancient times, myrrh was used as a tonic to purify the blood, and it may, of course, still be used to do the same thing. Vegetarians are always talking about the necessity of purifying the blood and getting the poisons out of the system, so if you decide that's what you'd like to do, myrrh is what you're after.

Nasturtiums

These wonderful flowers which may be used in salads and other foods also have medicinal value. They're good for urinary infections. And infusions made of the leaves are what the treatment calls for, and you want to be very sure you don't want to use antibiotics for this cure. The plant is antibiotic in a pure form, but you should see how quickly the urinary infection goes away. Since there is a variety of such infections, some of which lead to real damage if left untreated, you really do need to keep a watchful eye and consult the doctor immediately if all is not going well with the healing process.

Nutmeg

One of the wonderful memories I have of Grenada in the Caribbean in the old days was the sight of young children selling baskets of herbs on the beaches. They may still do that now, but it is most charming, and as far as herbal remedies go, you get a variety of them for a few dollars. Nutmeg is the only one I recognized from this Spice Island, but it is good to take if you have a lot of gas in your stomach. And if you've picked up one of the tourist diseases while traveling, you should try some nutmeg as it's said to curb nausea. You will want to be careful not to take too much, as if too much is taken, it is toxic and will leave you dizzy and with a possible loss of memory or some hallucinations. Just a very little bit should be taken, and a visit to the doctor is recommended if you need strong safe medication for diarrhea and other symptoms you have from drinking impure water. But however dangerous nutmeg can be, it is fragrant, and can cheer up the household with its aroma.

Oak

Here is a tree that's being used for herbal cures. The bark is the part that is used and boiling it makes an excellent gargle, or as a powder, it makes a fine remedy for nosebleed. It's such a powerful medication that it was used for tanning leather at one time, so you must be aware of what a strong decoction can be made from oak. It's also a good remedy for cuts or burns when used as a poultice. If you have a sore throat, gargle with it. If the sore throat doesn't go away, then ascertain whether you've got the common cold or bronchitis. If it's the latter, then take an antibiotic that the doctor prescribes.

Oat

Can you imagine it? Oat is good for depression! There's no need to be afraid of oat as a food and medication, although it can cause headaches if you overdose yourself on it. There are a lot of medications these days that are being used to treat depression by the medical establishment. If you have the kind of depression that makes you suicidal and is chronic and lasts for months at a time, you should be in the hands of a good psychiatrist who can prescribe the wonder medications that now exist for treating the condition. But if you have just occasional depressions that last one or two days, you can, without question, make yourself feel better by eating oat. The plant and seed are the parts that work, and you might just as well eat them and try to be fancy and make a decoction or some oat tea. But you must be very cautious about analyzing the kind of depression you have as it is a treatable disease, and the suffering it engenders is just terrible.

Orange Blossom

Orange blossom tea is just the thing to take when you want to strengthen your heart and nerves. It's a very calming tea, and if you feel your heart is pounding more than it should, a sip of the tea may help. Be careful not to overindulge yourself, and you should get an herb doctor's opinion when you're fooling around with internal organs that are as important as the heart.

Orange Leaves

I've mentioned use of the orange, and it's very effective for abdominal pain. Again, you wouldn't want to just use orange to treat a serious abdominal pain not knowing what's causing it and without seeking medical advice. If it's just a sharp gas pain due to indigestion, then you may take orange leaves and make them into a tea, much as you would use mallow. But you need to be certain that what you're treating is just a passing pain in the stomach. If the pain lasts any length of time, ask your doctor what the problem is that's causing it.

Pansy

Good for arthritis, pansy can be applied as an ointment directly to the affected areas. It's an upper respiratory remedy and can be used for very bad colds and even bronchitis (though always see a doctor if you have this ailment). If you're under the care of a doctor who is using pansy, he may give it to you for high blood pressure. It's also good for your nerves, and if wild violets don't help, then perhaps pansy will. There seem to be no dangerous side effects from using pansy, but, as with all herbs, check your herbal doctor to see that you're taking the right dosage and are using it for the condition you have in mind.

Parsley

The wonderful plant, parsley, that decorates plates of food is also good for treating urinary infections. Its effect is diuretic and is good for treating fluid retention. The little plant additionally is known for refreshing the breath. I used to go to a New York restaurant that kept a bowl of parsley in place of the mints kept in other restaurants. In fact, parsley is such a strong breath freshener that it can actually combat garlic which one might have had in one's meal. So always remember the trick of taking parsley for bad breath. If you're pregnant, however, stay away from parsley as it's not good to use. Any herbal remedy good for the urinary tract should be avoided when pregnant.

Passion Flower

This remedy is good for use as a tranquilizer. It's not addictive, and you may find it more palatable to use it for calming your state of mind than any of the modern tranquilizers, which often have unpleasant side effects—like addiction. So if you want to try a tranquilizer that is not harmful, as far as anyone can tell, then try passion flower.

Peppermint

I've recommended peppermint, and it's especially good with colds. If you inhale the peppermint, it breaks up the congestion of a cold. But there's a warning with it that you need to heed. Don't inhale it too much as the effect can be detrimental. And you should never give it to small children. Another popular use of peppermint is as an oil for a back rub. You can make it into a balm and spread it generously on the sore muscles. This is a wonderful herb to have when you're treating a lover or husband. Nothing is as stimulating to a relationship as a good, fragrant back rub, and peppermint is just the herb to do the job. You use the flowering part of the herb to make your decoctions and balms, and it's a good change from Vicks Vaporub as a remedy.

Plantain

Plantain, if it's the broad leaf variety, can be very good for dealing with bee stings and other insect bites. Just apply the leaves directly to the area afflicted and crush them so they'll loose their fluids on the sting. You'll need herb doctor care if you decide to use the seeds without soaking them, because the plantain needs to be carefully prepared (as do its seeds) for eating. Plantains grow in abundance in the Caribbean and are sold in Latino food stores and bodegas here. So if you find broad-leafed plantain, you should keep it on hand for occasions when someone gets stung.

Plantain is also used by the Hispanic community to treat dysentery and throat conditions. I would recommend that a modern city dweller be medically treated for dysentery rather than go to an herb doctor because it's a very serious condition. But if you have need of a throat gargle, plantain would be enormously helpful.

Pomegranate

Pomegranates grow in California and many areas of the tropics, so you have to use them on the East Coast as an important herbal remedy. They're very good for tonsilitis. And if you have a child with infected tonsils, you might want to try pomegranate before having a surgeon remove them. The pomegranate is boiled into a tea and you take it from there. Try a bit of tea several times a day and you may find a clearing up of the tonsil condition before the need arises to have them removed. Pomegranates aren't sweet; they have an unusual taste, so you may wish to add some honey to your tea. Honey can generally be added as a sweetener to various teas that are made of bland or sour fruits.

Potatoes

This is a very well-known remedy in parts of the South and Midwest. I have heard mention of it numerous times from people who knew I was gathering remedies for this book. What they say to do is cut the potato in half and rub it on your forehead. It's good for headache, which the potato takes away.

Northern Prickly Ash

Under medical supervision, the bark and berries of the ash may be used to treat arthritis. They promote the flow of blood to all parts of the body and are a tonic to the digestive system. While there are no cases of adverse effect with the use of the ash, it is wise to consult an herbal doctor to find out what kind of dosage you need to treat either your arthritis or digestive system. Ash can also be used to promote sweating during the course of an illness, and that helps break the fever. But my use of the ash is as an arthritis agent. I have a touch of arthritis in my left hip which was broken twelve years ago, and I've used ash to treat the arthritis emanating from this old accident. It does very well at reducing the pain. Since aspirin is prescribed in a great many cases for arthritis, I think that the prickly ash does just as effective a job, and of course eliminates the side effects of taking too much aspirin. Always check with your herbal doctor before you treat anything important to see if you've chosen the correct remedy at the correct dosage.

Evening Primrose

I recommend primrose for a number of conditions, but as an oil, it's also good for a variety of disorders. One of the most interesting remedies is for a hangover. And it is said that the liver, damaged by alcoholism, may begin the process of healing with the use of primrose. You don't want to take this remedy if you're epileptic, and it can cause side effects such as skin rashes. So you want to be careful about your dosage, and even have an herb doctor tell you how much is good for you. Be very careful when taking these home remedies as you can easily overdose yourself and become poisoned by an innocent-seeming herb.

Ragweed

I haven't mentioned ragweed as it is so allergy active. But if you aren't allergic, you can use it to make a very fine douche. Sometimes the weeds are better remedies than regular herbs, as in this case, so use it if you feel you'd like to try something different in the way of a natural douche.

Rose

I've recommended the rose as an antidote to a good many conditions. It makes a wonderful tea that soothes the internal system. Be sure to use rosehips to make the tea, as other varieties of rose are used for different reasons, especially pot-pourri and candy made from rosehips, etc. There are no dangerous side effects that I know of (always use extreme caution when you take something internally) and it is a very pleasant balm for your insides at the end of a busy day.

Rosemary

Aside from being a delicious herb to cook with, rosemary also has some medicinal properties. It may be used for headaches and digestion (indigestion). Oil of rosemary is what you want to use on your headache. Apply it to your forehead, or take it as an infusion. But you must remember that with rosemary, you must not take the oil directly as it is powerful and may bring on illness. Stay away from drinking the pure oil of rosemary. Take some of the herb leaves for your digestive tract if you feel the need. You can put them in with your food and have the benefit of the herb in your cooking as well as its remedial qualities.

Rue

You will need to make or purchase an ointment that contains the rue plant (you use the parts that are above ground). The purpose of the ointment is to treat sprains. You need an herbal doctor to advise you on the dosage for any of the uses of rue, as it is very powerful and can be poisonous. The ointment that you make is also good for rheumatic pain, but it's best for sprains and bruises. If you have an emergency and no ointment prepared, you can try making a poultice of the plant and that should bring some relief. I can't give you much advice about this herbal remedy, as when I come across a poisonous one when taken in the wrong dosage, I tend to stay away from it; and I would advise you to do the same. I just don't think the risk is justified.

Rue is also good for earache. Mix it with Vaseline, then gently put it in your ear. The ache hopefully will vanish within a short period. You'll want to use dried rue, or a decoction of fresh rue to make your ointment. If the earache continues, by all means see your doctor.

Sage

Here is another herb widely used in cooking that also has medicinal properties. Sore throat is one of the conditions sage cures, as well as menstrual problems. You may make a gargle of it for your sore throat, and it can also be used as a tea. You may take the tea for cramps that may develop with your menstrual period. There is a warning about sage tea however. It shouldn't be taken for more than a week at a time with a long period of rest between weeks. There's a possible toxic effect with some of the properties of sage if it's used too often.

Sarsaparilla

Sarsaparilla is also a home remedy, and is especially good for psoriasis and as a purifier of the blood. The root is the important part of this plant. Boiled, it will produce the substance needed for curing psoriasis, though you may find that there is very little that can be done with a severe case. So using sarsaparilla on the problem may just make a difference in how it heals.

Saw Palmetto

Take a little bit of saw palmetto and, under doctor's orders, you can treat a condition of impotence. It's the berries that are the parts of the plant you want to use. It's also recommended as a treatment for infertility in the female and as an all-around tonic for the body. There are no serious warnings that go with saw palmetto, but as in all of these herbal remedies, someone with an herbal background—a homeopathic doctor or other person knowledgeable about home remedies—should be on hand to guide your usage and teach you more about the herb.

Shepherd's Purse

Shepherd's purse is a plant that may be eaten as a vegetable, as can many of the herbal remedies, and is also used as a fine home remedy for varicose veins. I recommend it for that purpose, and you make a poultice of the leaves and wrap them around your legs over the veins. Another use of this plant is as an herb to stop bleeding. If you are menstruating too much or too long, try taking some of the purse as a vegetable. If you find yourself heavily menstruating and this is not your normal pattern, always check the doctor before using shepherd's purse to stop it. A change in menstrual patterns may mean trouble, so you should always have yourself checked if something unusual is occurring. But I'd suggest using it most for varicose veins as there is little trouble you can get into with the herb as a poultice. My best advice is always to be more timid than self-assured around home remedies and you will usually do well.

Silver Birch

Silver birch is good for arthritis, and its young leaves also treat infections. Make into a tea, and drink no more than two cups a day. I use silver birch to treat the arthritis that Jim, my Indian friend, has in his shoulders and foot. He isn't using the painkillers that his doctor gave him though because he turned out to be allergic to them and blotches came out all over his legs. So now, instead of using the prescribed painkillers, I rely on silver birch. He says that while it doesn't take away all the pain, he can tell the difference and it makes him feel somewhat better.

Skunk Cabbage

While I haven't talked about skunk cabbage as a remedy in the last section (because it smells so awful), it is indeed used as a medication. People use the root of skunk cabbage to cure coughs of varying seriousness. But, as always, I wouldn't recommend using this remedy for an upper respiratory ailment which requires antibiotics. It might be a good way to ease smoker's cough or a cough leading to a head cold, but for the serious disease, no. Skunk cabbage has some sedative qualities, but I certainly wouldn't use it as I do chamomile tea.

Soapwort

This herb is used like soap, and indeed it is good for skin conditions. It's good for psoriasis, which really can't be treated effectively by modern medications. My older brother in Hawaii has psoriasis all over his legs and is now treating it with medication his doctor prescribed—and is also trying soapwort externally, as it is somewhat poisonous. Just use it on those skin conditions that won't respond well to medication, and it just might be that a treatment of soapwort is all that was needed to clear up your disease.

Spasm Herb

Hispanics use spasm herb for infection and drink it as a tea. If you have an infection, you might try spasm herb which you can, no doubt, get in botanicas which are herb stores catering to Latinos. You'll want to check with your herb doctor to make certain that what you're using is correct, and then try it out.

Spurge

Spurge is good for the removal of warts, although the best medication I've found is Compound W. But spurge is the herbal way to remove them, and if your doctor says that it's not worth taking them off, try some spurge and do it yourself. I have a lot of warts that have appeared in the last few years, and my doctor told me they were hereditary and not cancerous or dangerous in any way. I don't know if spurge will remove hereditary warts, but it's good for common ones that you pick up as a viral infection. Don't overdo the spurge tea because spurge is a powerful plant and you don't want side effects from it that might make you ill.

Stinging Nettle

This plant is found everywhere and can be used for a variety of conditions. It's good for arthritis and should be made into a tea to effect a remedy. It also can be applied, like a poultice, directly on the arthritic limb. Stinging nettles, in addition, are good for heavy menstruation, and help stop bleeding. There are a few other conditions nettles are good for, but the most helpful ones are here. You must be careful about using the nettles as they prick your fingers and cause tiny spots of pain. You should use gloves when handling them or, better yet, buy them at the herb emporium already fixed into medication. You use the leaf and stem of this plant to make your remedies.

Swamp Root

This plant can be made into a tea to treat stomach troubles. If you're gassy and need treatment for that, try swamp root to see if that helps. Chances are if you have stomach problems that take you the medication route, you'll want to consult a doctor and perhaps take some tests if the condition is something more than simple indigestion. I have a friend who currently is going through tests to check problems with her stomach. I wouldn't recommend swamp root to her at this point as what's wrong with her is not known. But if she had simple indigestion and didn't want to take Alka Seltzer or Pepto Bismol or any of the other home remedy standbys, then I'd recommend a tea of swamp root and see if she felt any better.

Tansy Mustard

I haven't emphasized tansy as a remedy because there are so many other herbs that do the same thing and just as well. But no herbal book would be complete without the mention of tansy, I've decided, so here it is. Tansy mustard tea is good for indigestion. It is also used sometimes for infection, but I'd want a doctor's opinion on that. If you're trying different herbal remedies for a stomachache caused by indigestion, then tansy is among the ones to try.

Thyme

Oil of thyme is something you don't want to mix without a professional homeopathic doctor who knows something about herbs. It can be poisonous. But thyme used as a tea is very good with sore throats. I've fixed it myself and find it very soothing. If you have a cold and cough beyond just the sore throat, you'll find that thyme tea is most beneficial. You don't want to take more than two cups a day, as like any of these herbs, too much can be dangerous. Thyme tea is also good for your digestive system. The dangerous oil can be used as a rubbing solution, so that you can have someone rub your back and chest with it if you have a cold. It's especially good for rheumatism, so if you know someone with that complaint, you can give them a treatment with the oil.

Tomato

A tomato is said to work similarly to a potato to cure a sore throat. Make a poultice of it and wrap it around your neck. You will begin to feel better, especially if you use one of the gargles recommended earlier.

Valerian

I've talked about valerian and its many good uses, but it's especially helpful for nervous conditions. You'll want to consult your herb doctor about the taking of valerian as too much of it can cause unpleasant side effects including terrible headaches. Nervousness may be treated with this herb, but don't use it over long periods as the side effects are very bad, possibly making worse the condition you already have. It's the valerian root that is used in making remedies, and a tea may be made of it to cure what ails you.

Vervain

This plant may be used as a cure for migraine headaches as well as depression. You must admit to yourself, first, however, that the depression isn't a result of alcohol consumption but in reality is just a simple depression that sometimes comes on. Vervain is a fine remedy for exhaustion brought on by nerves, and you can use the leaves to treat yourself. You need to get herbal medical advice on just what to use for what with this plant, and there is a warning not to use the herb when you're pregnant. There are a lot of home remedies as well as prescribed medications that cannot be used during pregnancy, so it is important to follow directions about these.

Violet

I've recommended violets for a variety of conditions and they're especially good for respiratory ones. Stay away from the roots and seeds which quite possibly can cause side effects. But the flower can be used for headaches by applying the violets directly on the throbbing spot. The flowers are also sedative, and you can make a tea of the plants.

Watercress

This herb is like so many others in that it's good as a home remedy for a variety of conditions, especially for coughs and arthritis, and its stems and leaves make wonderful salads and watercress sandwiches for teas. You can make a poultice of watercress that you wrap around your arthritic joints. And some advocates of the properties of herbs and plants choose watercress to stimulate and use its expectorant qualities to treat coughs that may have become bronchitis. As you can tell by now, I never recommend just herbs and other plants for serious conditions such as bronchitis. I've had bronchitis a number of times and realize that the only remedy is the correct antibiotic. So a cough caused by smoking may bend to the ministrations of an herbalist treating you for it with watercress, but I would be very hesitant to recommend a treatment for bronchitis with just this herb.

Wild Lettuce

This plant may be used to relieve anxiety. Make a soothing tea of the leaves, and see how relaxed you get. It is also a fine remedy for a cigarette cough. I suffer from anxiety from time to time and I make tea to soothe my nerves. You never really are able to identify anxiety easily because it causes such stomach pain that you think something physical is wrong with you. If you take a remedy for anxiety, you suddenly find that your stomach relaxes and you aren't constantly battling the pain you didn't realize was anxiety. I feel that anxiety is a root cause for people turning to alcohol for medication. The trouble is that, as a remedy, alcohol is a dangerous drug and should be shunned in favor of other cures. Identifying the anxiety that may cause you to take up drinking is very important, and if you try a cup of tea made from wild lettuce and it soothes your nerves, then you can pretty well discover that it's been anxiety you've been doing battle with.

Willow

I haven't mentioned willow before as it's one of those plants that may or may not cause bad reactions. The trick is to take just a little of it in a tea and you should be all right. If this makes you nervous, then ask your herb doctor about it. Willow tea is good for fevers, so a call to your herb doctor wouldn't be amiss anyway. You just don't let fevers go on for very long without checking to see why you have one.

White Willow

This tree bark is also very effective for arthritis. Your herbal doctor may prescribe this for you instead of prickly ash. The bark contains substances very much like those found in aspirin, and your doctor may feel you would benefit from the white willow. Try to buy the bark, as it is not always easy to prepare fresh barks in the home. You must boil it for about twenty minutes, in some cases longer. And you always want to be absolutely sure that you can take the result internally or should apply it outside as a poultice. But this bark, as it's so close to aspirin, may be taken internally with the right dosage prescribed by your herbal doctor.

Witch Hazel

I haven't mentioned the use of witch hazel very much so far, but I'll recommend it for varicose veins. All you need to do is make a poultice of the leaves and bark and apply it to your varicose veins for fifteen or twenty minutes at a sitting. I swear by the witch hazel that's like alcohol and is a much more subtle substance than rubbing alcohol. So I'm certain that fresh witch hazel used in a poultice is just the right concoction to make. It's also very good for bruises if you happen to have bad ones that needs some kind of treatment. You should put a witch hazel poultice on it and it will soothe the sting out of the bruise.

Wormseed

This herb is good for a stomachache and can be made into a tea. It's also good for a simple pain in the stomach, but who would not go to a doctor immediately with a terrible stomach pain. If it's just a gassy stomachache from overeating, then take some wormseed tea. But if you have a condition you can't diagnose, see someone who can and don't take the wormseed tea till given the okay by a doctor.

Wormwood

I've told you about the properties of wormwood, but it's good as a remedy for worms and as a tonic. Internally, as a tonic, it seems to have the effect of regulating the appetite. If your child develop worms, and the doctor doesn't prescribe anything that is more than an over-the-counter remedy, then you may ask him about using wormwood. If he is familiar with herbal remedies, he may agree to its use. In fact, you must choose your doctor carefully when you're looking to take care of a condition usually treated with modern medication because he probably won't know much about home remedies. You'd need to choose a homeopathic doctor, or one sensitive to regional uses of home medicines such as the Southwest or southern states. Be aware that wormwood is on the dangerous medicines list of the Food and Drug Administration, so don't use this at all without proper medical supervision.

Wild Yam

The root of the wild yam is what you want to use for menstrual cramps and arthritis. If you are afflicted with terrible cramps, then the wild yam may be the answer for you—as an antispasmodic plant—and its cure is good for a number of conditions which require the calming physical influence of a plant such as this. It's also recommended for a time in pregnancy that a miscarriage may occur. But I would see how it affects the terrible cramping that one gets at the time of menstruation, and that cure may make the wild yam a valuable ally in your array of herbal medicines.

III

Illnesses That Herbs Can Cure

RHEUMATISM

Cayenne

I've mentioned the use of cayenne before and its cure of increasing the blood flow to areas of the body that have arthritis or rheumatism. You use the fruit of cayenne to create either poultices or liniment, but you must avoid prolonged usage as it is hard on the skin and may cause problems. Too much consumption can produce gastroenteritis and lead to kidney problems. If you're going to use cayenne, I recommend consulting an herb doctor for the correct dosage. You are just not smart to use this remedy for too long without medical advice, as the side effects (such as kidney damage) are severe.

Celery

The parts used in the celery for remedies are the root, leaves, and seeds, and you make a juice of these to be used for rheumatism. While there are no warnings that come with overuse of celery, you certainly don't want to take too much (perhaps a few glasses a day) as too much of a good thing always seem to produce side effects. You need to use your head when you make your own remedies for health conditions, as mistakes can easily be made that cause more damage then you're trying to cure.

Centaury

This plant may be made into an infusion or powder, and again, it's good for rheumatism and joint pains. There are few side effects but you may wish to make a tea and drink it several times a day. You can also make a poultice for aching joints and leave that on for twenty minutes or so.

Cinnamon

Another common herb found in most pantrys and is good for treating colds can also be used for rheumatism and arthritis. The cinnamon part you use is the bark, common in most herb stores. You powder the bark and make a tea, or make an infusion. In any case, cinnamon is the herb of choice after a rugged day on the ski slopes or in other winter settings, and it should be put in a glass of hot cider. It's also a wonderful additive to iced tea in the summer and imparts a gentle, soothing flavor. So you may actually be treating rheumatism and arthritis while you're having a social drink.

Dandelion

I've mentioned this plant (weed) quite a few times, but its recommended use is for chronic rheumatism. You can use the leaves and roots to make tea, and not be concerned about side effects unless you're allergic to dandelions.

Fennel

I've mentioned fennel before but not specifically in conjunction with rheumatism. The parts of the plant that are used are the root, seeds, and leaves, and they can be made into a decoction or an infusion. It's for external use only, so you need to turn the decoction or infusion into a poultice to use on the joint.

Garlic

I've talked about garlic before too, but not specifically for rheumatism. Make the bulb into a juice or tea, or even eat it raw. I don't know of anyone who could use it more often than that, due to its odor, but as a tea or juice, you may take it once a day and see if the effect is worth the smell.

Horseradish

I've also mentioned horseradish, but it is a wonderful remedy for arthritis or rheumatism. Use the fresh root to make a decoction, poultice, or juice. You can have a choice as to what form in which you want to take it. There are no terrible side effects from horseradish, so you may want to try it twice a day. You'll have to experiment with the different remedies if you have rheumatism or painful arthritis to see which one works best for you. You may wish to do this under an herb doctor's supervision. That way, you won't be so nervous taking these plants and herbs that are basically, still, so little known in this country.

Red Clover

Here's an herb in which you use the flower to make a fomentation. You may also make a poultice of these and place them on your rheumatic limb. As a fomentation, you may use it to treat gout, although fooling around with this condition is dangerous as excess uric acid can get in your bloodstream. Gout needs to be treated professionally. But the flowers of red clover make a very fine treatment for rheumatism.

Rosemary

Leaves and flowers of the rosemary herb may be used to make a salve to treat rheumatism. You don't want to ingest this herb in quantity as it can be poisonous, but turned into a rub for arthritic and rheumatic limbs works very nicely.

Rue

This is another common cooking herb that has a dangerous side. Too much of it can cause poisoning. But if you use the tops of young plants and make it into an ointment, you'll find it's another very fine remedy for rheumatism.

Sarsaparilla

Use the root stalk and make an infusion. This too is good for rheumatism and may be taken internally. As with all herbs, even the common cooking ones have safety zones for ingestion. Some are just better used as ointments rather than taken internally.

Thyme

Make an oil of thyme and use it on limbs that are rheumatic. There are no terrible warnings about thyme as there are about rue and rosemary, but you still want to take care. Thyme can be made into an infusion as well as an oil, but I would recommend the latter as the better remedy. It just seems like putting oil on a sore spot should have a better and faster effect than taking a dose of liquid. So with arthritis and rheumatism, I go for the oils and poultices that can be made with ease and used at will.

Willow

I've mentioned willow and the parts you use are the bark and leaves to make a decoction or a cold extract or even a powder. All these are rheumatic remedies, and the chemicals that can be found in willow are close to those you find in aspirin. Of course, if you're not taking aspirin or other medications the doctor orders for rheumatism and arthritis, it's likely that it's because you're allergic to them. Even if you're not, you are trying a variety of dangerous herbs as self-remedies to treat your condition. Stay with the less dangerous ones and be careful about ingesting even those.

ANTISPASMODICS

Spasms and convulsions may be treated by the antispasmodics listed below. If you ever have conditions like these, find out from your doctor what he recommends for use. If he prescribes a medication that could easily be foregone for a home remedy, then have your herb doctor advise you on the subject of antispasmodics. I offer some here for you to consider and to discuss with your herb doctor, if he wants to know what remedies you have in mind.

Balm

I'm in favor of the use of balm if the spasm you're experiencing is just a case of jumpy nerves. Balm may be made into a poultice, infusion, cold extract, or tincture, but I recommend the poultice. It's wonderfully comforting to the affected nerves to be wrapped in a poultice for about twenty minutes to half an hour.

Chamomile

Chamomile is used for many different conditions, and one of its strongest points is that it may be used for spasms. Spasms may come from medication prescribed by doctors who are treating mental conditions. The miracle drugs for the mentally ill don't come without side effects. There is an antispasmodic drug which is fine, so if you're able to control the side effect of using this remedy so much the better. Chamomile shouldn't be taken more than a few cups a day, and find out from your herb doctor if he would recommend it as a replacement for Cogentin.

Dill

This is another cooking herb which has effective use as a home remedy. It's an antispasmodic and can be used as an infusion or oil. The parts used are either dried or fresh greens. I'd use the latter as a poultice on affected parts, or mix the dill with oil and rub the spasm area. The powder would be the most effective with the oil, so you may wish to prepare some to have on hand.

Mullein

This plant is an excellent antispasmodic but, because of its properties, is somewhat sedative and slightly narcotic. The leaves and flowers are used and made into an infusion or tincture. I personally think tinctures are too strong unless made under the specific watchful eye of an herb doctor.

Orange

The fruit peel, leaves, and flowers are all recommended as helpful to convulsions. You need to take what the doctor prescribes for you for such a condition, but if you are all alone in some rural area and away from a doctor, and you are having convulsions or are with someone who is having them, then oranges should help in treating the condition.

Parsley

Good old parsley! Like chamomile, it turns up everywhere and is a safe and lovely herb to use as a home remedy. You can make a tea or decoction to treat spasms. When I say it's safe, it is for those people without kidney inflammation or other problems in that area. Never take parsley as a medicine if you have kidney problems.

Red Clover

Red clover is also highly reliable as an antispasmodic. The flowers are used as an infusion or tincture, and there are no dangerous side effects to contend with. Red clover is also known as trefoil in the Northeast, so that may help you to identify it. Try it when you have need of such a remedy and see if it isn't just what the herb doctor ordered.

Sweet Basil

Sweet basil made into an infusion or used as a dried herb is good for spasms as well. You might find out if it can be used to treat epilepsy, if you have it. Your herb doctor may, in fact, think sweet basil was a proper remedy, or perhaps has something else in mind that he's worked with. But it's worth keeping this herb around as it's also fine for cooking and you can serve it now and again so family and friends get the effect of its antispasmodic properties.

Valerian

Always use the root fresh in this herb and you may make an infusion or a cold extract of it. Valerian is well known as an antispasmodic, but before doing that, see that it's used properly, as large doses or extended use may cause symptoms of poisoning. To find the right dose for you, consult the herb doctor. He should be watching over you anyway as any illness with spasms should not be treated without advice from a qualified source.

ANTIDEPRESSANT

Marijuana

Marijuana is an illegal substance, but that doesn't stop it from being an antidepressant. Any book about herbs must mention it somewhere, and I have. I don't recommend that you use it as an antidepressant when there are so many fine drugs that may be prescribed for the condition. Marijuana's effect wears off quickly and isn't as powerful an antidote as, say, Elavil.

BRONCHODIALATORS

Cinnamon

Cinammon which was listed earlier is also a fine antidote to colds. Made into a tea and taken twice a day, it's very soothing on the chest when the cold has dropped down to that area. Use Vicks Vaporub if what you have is a regular cold. If you are able to drink, add a drop of alcohol to the cinnamon tea and that will help relax you as much as any prescribed medication. Just be careful not to keep on drinking the alcohol and putting yourself into a stupor that will probably lead to a hangover the next morning.

Garlic

Garlic comes up again as a fine antidote and this time it works wonders against whooping cough and acts as expectorant. Use it for colds that have traveled to your chest, perhaps in place of prescribed cough medicine (if you can't take drugs). Garlic shouldn't be overused, but two cups a day would be enough to help relieve your condition.

Oregano

Good for the respiratory system as well as for coughs and colds is oregano made into a tea. It sets well as an expectorant and for coughs. You may use dried oregano, but it's best to use fresh, either grown by you or purchased at a health food store. Growing your own herbs is really the best way to keep track of them, but if there's an herb store you trust, especially in the big city, then you can use its services. It's good to know that oregano, used extensively in Italian cooking, is also right for remedying ailments of the upper respiratory system.

Sage

Sage, another well-known cooking herb, should not be used during pregnancy and should be used carefully for anyone with a condition that needs treating. It's good for coughs, and is officially known as red sage. If you do have a cough, then take some fresh, or even dried, sage and make a tea of it. Drink no more than two cups a day, and if you want further advice (especially if you're pregnant and shouldn't use it at all), call your herb doctor and get his view.

Spearmint

Spearmint, which is also known as Yerba Buena, can be used for a cold and in tea form. You're not supposed to drink too much of this herb either, so try two cups a day. There are so many wonderful remedies for the common cold that it's surprising how little is known about them. With the medical profession knowing so little about what to prescribe for colds, you should go ahead and use your folk remedies to treat them. The cough medicine prescribed by doctors most often has narcotic substances in it, and if you want to be sure you're not getting any, try one of these teas and you'll feel better without the worry that they're dangerous to you.

CARDIOVASCULAR SYSTEM

The herbs listed below are especially good for lowering high blood pressure and as diuretics. These are some of the conditions for which doctors also prescribe. In fact, there are so many diuretics and high blood pressure medications on the market that don't work without side effects, you should ask your doctor if you can try any of the herbs in their stead. Your herb doctor will help you with the dosage and your regular physician, while not being particularly happy about your decision, may give you the go-ahead to try one of these before using his medications.

Alfalfa

Alfalfa is a plant that can help combat high blood pressure and is also good for blood clotting because of the vitamin K in it. The alfalfa leaves are used to make tea or an infusion, and you may have two or three cups a day of the tea. If you're a hemophiliac, you might try asking an herb doctor about taking alfalfa tea for the condition, as it clots blood. And if you're going in for surgery, ask the herb doctor if alfalfa tea might be good to take ahead of time so that your blood will have the assistance of the vitamin K to help it clot during the operation.

Borage

Leaves and flowers of borage make a diuretic that you might like to try. It can be made as an infusion, which I recommend, or as a poultice. Take two cups of borage a day and see if it works. If not, ask your herb doctor what he thinks about more than twice a day and go to it.

Epsom Salts

Epsom salts are a true home remedy that can be found on the shelves of every drugstore—a wonderful laxative that also lowers high blood pressure. You don't want to take epsom salts too frequently, however, as pain and weaknesses in the legs may develop. Otherwise, just follow the directions on the label and you'll be all right.

Foxglove

A cup of foxglove tea is what you should take for congestive heart disease if you suffer from that condition. It has digitalis in it and is often used in the South and Southwest where people go to clinics that specialize not only in modern medical techniques but also in home remedies. These home remedy recipes have been passed on through the generations and are talked about in books such as this one. Unless you're going to one of these clinics, you probably will be prescribed digitalis in another form (most likely a pill) if that's what the doctor orders. But if you're alone in a rural area and your heart condition acts up, then you'll know what to take—foxglove tea.

Garlic

Garlic pops up all over the place, this time as a diuretic when taken in tea or juice form, or even raw. The garlic is also known as a reducer of high blood pressure. Because of its odor, you may want to forego taking much garlic. And I've read a recipe for garlic soup that might be better, as when you boil the herb, the odor subsides. But you'll have to figure out just how much garlic you should take at any given time. I'd say two or three cloves twice a day. If you're going to use it as a diuretic or blood pressure medication, I'd check with the herb doctor to see what he suggests as a dosage.

Ginger

Ginger is a strong stimulant in the circulatory system and should be made into a tea using the root. I wouldn't take this more than twice a day as it's strong medication. While no dire side effects accompany this herb, it seems to me that you should probably take advice from your herb doctor about how much ginger root to use. I'd say several peels but he may want you to take more, or less, for your condition.

Honey and Lemon Tea

You wouldn't think that honey and lemon could do very much as home remedies, but, in fact, they're used to regulate blood pressure and as a diuretic. You may want to ask your physician if it's okay to take honey and lemon while on a prescribed diuretic or pill to lower blood pressure (which are often the same medications). With his permission, take several tablespoons of honey with several of lemon and mix and drink. I've used honey and lemon as a diuretic and it's very helpful and quite good. Try it, too, and see if this doesn't become one of your favorite remedies.

Mesquite Leaves

You may try these as a diuretic and make them into a tea. You will have to order these, and a good place to ask about them are the restaurants, generally in the Southwest, serving foods cooked by mesquite, or in an herb store. They may have some leaves that came with their logs. Check with your herb doctor about the number of leaves you should use to make the tea.

Tea and Coffee

Both tea and coffee are strong stimulants and diuretic in effect. If you're going to drink either of these for that purpose, I'd check the herb doctors or even a physician about how much to imbibe in any one day. Too much tea may not be good for you, even as too much coffee certainly isn't. I drink about six or seven cups of coffee a day at the office, and I know how diuretic its effect is, as well as how much of a stimulant. For the sake of good health, you're not supposed to take more than two or three cups of coffee a day, but that hasn't stopped me. I'm just addicted to it and don't want to let it go right now. The English, who take quite a bit of strong tea, should be aware of how much they're drinking as it contains substances that shouldn't be ingested too often. So our favorite morning and afternoon brews carry warnings with them and we really should abide by them.

Yellow Root

This root also is for high blood pressure. Make a tea of it, but don't drink more than two cups a day unless the doctor prescribes another dosage. And you might experiment to see if you prefer yellow root to some of the other blood pressure stabilizers that have been mentioned here. There are so many treatments for the condition that you should be able to find one that suits you. Try yellow root to see if this is the right herb for you.

GASTROINTESTINAL

Gastrointestinal conditions may be treated with herbs used for other conditions as well. For example, carminative remedies get rid of gas in the stomach, while some others work well on ulcers. And still others are just good for keeping digestive acids under control. So if you have conditions from indigestion to peptic ulcers, these remedies can help.

Alfalfa

Mentioned before, for its blood clotting properties, alfalfa is also good for helping to cure peptic ulcers. It contains vitamins K, A, C, D, and E and helps with the digestive stomach acid with its soothing qualities. Make it into a tea or juice and enjoy one or two cups a day of this healthy home remedy.

Cayenne

Cayenne again is another remedial guise, this time in an infusion, used to stimulate gastric secretions. It helps you digest your food if your gastric juices aren't just right. Cayenne will stimulate your stomach, and it's also another fine carminative (good for a gassy problem). If you feel bloated over a long period after eating, you may wish to try the cayenne to see if it helps. You had best check with an herb store to see if you can get cayenne easily.

Chamomile

Good old chamomile is good both for controlling gas and as a sedative. Make it into a tea or as an infusion if you like. It can also be made into a poultice to place over your stomach, or it works well as an oil. In any case, chamomile has many uses and very few bad side effects if handled properly and in the right quantities.

Cinnamon

This is fine for a tonic that warms and soothes your digestive system. Make cinnamon tea and enjoy how you feel—relaxed and ready for a snooze. Cinnamon has a long history of being good for the digestive tract. Just think of all the hot toddies with cinnamon sticks in which people with colds have inbibed to make them feel better. It's just a fine, all-around home remedy to have on hand for occasions when stress has your stomach in knots or you feel gassy. Yup, it's good for that too.

Cumin

This is a common cooking herb used as a remedy for indigestion, gas, digestive problems in children, and menstrual cramps. Such a common herb to have so much power! You make a tea of the cumin seeds, either ground or whole—it doesn't matter. And I wouldn't take more than two teas a day unless otherwise recommended by an herb doctor, since cumin in quantity is quite powerful.

Garlic

Here's garlic again which, with chamomile, heads the list of useful home remedies. This time garlic, which may be taken raw, as a juice or as a tea, is good both for stomach ulcers and for destroying intestinal worms. Worms are common in children who occasionally put dirty things in their mouths. But worms in adults are rarer. There's medication for worms from your doctor, but if you want to try curing it at home, use garlic.

Ginger

You wouldn't think that ginger would be good for much beyond flavoring cookies, but it is therapeutic as well. Ginger is a carminative remedy which means that it's good for gassy stomachs. I have a friend who is trying the ginger cure for a serious case of gas, and says that there has been a change for the better. I certainly hope so, as there are few more embarrassing bodily functions in public than passing gas.

Honey and Lemon

This delicious remedy, used for several complaints, is also good for the gastrointestinal system when it becomes upset. It's antiseptic and will help kill unwanted bacteria in your digestive system. If you suffer from gassy stomach pains, take some honey and lemon and see if you don't feel better. I recently visited a close friend in the hospital who was waiting to be operated on for diverticulitis. This condition is caused by pockets forming in the colon that trap food. The colon becomes inflamed and infected. My friend had severe stomach pains before she was hospitalized, and decided that the condition was worsening and wouldn't respond well to home remedies. I'm glad she made the decision not to rely on honey and lemon to cure the pains as she soon was in a quite serious condition, with tubes running out of her nose and neck. She is as good an example as any for letting modern medicine work when it's needed. Home remedies can't be relied on to cure very serious illness, and don't let anyone talk you into believing differently. Herbs and home cures have their place, but not with a life-threatening condition.

Mint

Mint tea is very good for stimulating your stomach and strengthening it—a stomachic. You can grow your own mint or buy it at an herb store, and use it in other drinks beside tea. Mint is especially good in iced tea, and mint juleps are traditional in the South. Mint is not toxic in any way, so you can have more than just a few teas during the day without fear. And as I say, if you feel any weakness in the stomach, take mint for the feeling and the distress will soon go away.

Mugwort

Used as an infusion, it is able to shrink hemorroids and prevent formation of internal abscesses. Excess dosage may lead to symptoms of poisoning like all members of the genus mugwort. It is not to be used if pregnancy is suspected. There's a fine hemorrhoidal medication, Preparation H, on the market which does well; otherwise, try mugwort for shrinking hemorrhoids.

Olive Oil

Here's a remedy using olive oil that I bet you never considered: It's good to combat constipation. It seems this is a very individual condition and not all laxatives work the same way in all people. But if you take a tablespoonful of olive oil, you won't go wrong. Mineral oil is another laxative to try, and goes back to our grandmother's days. Any oil should produce some laxative effect, but these two are recommended through long experience. I always make certain that my diet contains some margarine for that reason. I don't think having no fat in the diet is a good idea, so I always have margarine during the day. You must just use common sense in these matters, and if you do get constipated on occasion, try one of the oils as a sound remedy.

Orange

Oranges turn out to be home remedies, too. They help adjust the digestive system to rid your body of extra gas. Orange is a tonic, too, that encourages the digestive system to work efficiently. One in the morning is a fine way to start the day, and, of course, juice, pressed from fresh oranges, is as effective as the whole fruit. All parts of the orange may be used to make a remedy. The leaves and flowers, fruit, and peel all help the stomach. Those with orange trees in their backyards are blessed indeed and will be able to relate to this digestive aid at once.

Oregano

As an infusion, oregano can clear up an upset stomach and indigestion. I simply wouldn't go to all the trouble of making it when all you have to do is take an Alka Seltzer or Tums and the indigestion is gone. With these readily accessible medications, you also get the added benefits of calcium, and as you get older, you need to add calcium to your diet to prevent osteoporosis. A Tums a day, as they say, keeps the doctor away.

Rose

Rose can be used for a multitude of conditions, but here, as a tea, it makes a fine stomachic (which strengthens the stomach) as a purge and a laxative. Because rose tea is so marvelous, I recommend that you go to the trouble of making it up if you need some laxative or just want to purge your stomach. Several cups of rose tea a day will do the trick for you.

Rue

As an infusion, oil, or tincture, rue is used for stomachaches and antiseptic purposes. Be aware, however, that large doses may cause poisoning. Contact with the plant can cause skin irritation, and the juice is an irritant and should not be used by pregnant women. With that warning, use it carefully and you'll be all right. Rue is used in cooking in small doses, but as a home remedy it can be poisonous. Get medical advice if you decide to use it.

Sage

Sage tea, ingested to relieve gastric distress, should be avoided by women who are pregnant. For the rest, you should drink no more than two cups of sage tea a day, as it's a very powerful medication and should be used with respect. I doubt that anyone will ever convince me that sage tea should replace Alka Seltzer in my medicine chest, but I'm willing to try it the next time my stomach acts up just to see what the effect is. Since I rarely have stomach problems, I may have to rely on others to report on how the sage tea worked for them.

Soda Bicarbonate

My grandmother gave me soda bicarbonate when I stayed overnight at her house as a youngster and I had a stomachache. She diagnosed me as having eaten too many sweets and out came the bicarbonate. If you're in your forties or fifties, you probably have similar stories to tell. It's still just as fine a remedy as it always was, so try it yourself even if you haven't got a grandmother with a reassuring and soothing teaspoon of bicarbonate.

Swallow Wort

Use this as a poultice to wrap around your stomach. It's antimicrobic and antiseptic and will bring soothing feelings to an overwrought digestive system.

Sweet Basil

This cooking herb can be used in dried herb form or as an infusion for stomach problems such as spasms and gastric distress. There are no warnings that it causes problems when used with other medications, and as long as you take it twice a day, and no more, without a doctor's orders to do so. Over-the-counter medication is also available for problems that basil can remedy.

GYNECOLOGICAL

Aloe

The aloe, especially good with cuts and burns, is an emmenagogue, which means that it brings on the menstrual period if it's behind schedule. This is particularly true of the aloe if taken as a powder or pill. So it's fine to take to bring on the menses, but dangerous if you're pregnant. If you're doing herbal remedies and have a doctor who is familiar with most of them, then get his opinion on any herb that you are thinking of using, especially if it has a warning with it in books like this. Your doctor will be able to verify the danger if there is one, and you'll be more relaxed when taking it. Meanwhile, stay away from aloe if you're pregnant.

Chamomile

I laugh as I add chamomile to the gynecological remedies available. Chamomile is so good for many maladies that you should have the tea on hand at all times. It's good for cramps as a soothing tonic in tea form. Incidentally, chamomile is also known as Manzanilla, so if you see it as that, you'll know it's the real thing under another name.

Cumin

Cumin is an abortifacient and should be avoided if you're pregnant. How powerful and strong an abortifacient these herbs are is beside the point. It may not take much to induce labor prematurely and cause an abortion.

Oregano

Here is another herb to regulate the menstrual cycle that should not be taken when pregnant. A little sprinkled in food probably wouldn't hurt you, but I wouldn't even take that. You take the oregano as an infusion, and after several days, the cycle should be restored. But it shouldn't be taken by pregnant women who have no need for it anyway. If you want to take oregano for something else, check with your herb doctor first.

Rue

The reason rue and other herbs that I've mentioned shouldn't be used by pregnant women is because they promote the menstrual cycle and, in some cases, are abortifacients. Rue is one such abortifacient and should never be used when pregnancy is suspected.

Spearmint

Spearmint turns up as a good solid herb for various ailments, and here is another: it helps stop menstrual cramps. There are lots of over-the-counter drugs you can get for this condition, and, since there are so many of these remedies, it means the doctors and pharmaceutical companies haven't really found the all-around cure for cramps. Spearmint might be just the ticket. Try it and see if it works well on you. I rarely had cramps as a young woman so I never had to resort to remedies, but I know lots who did suffer and I'm certain there are many who might try the spearmint. If I had a problem, I certainly would.

EYE, EAR, NOSE, AND THROAT

Aloe, in tea form, is suggested for use as an eyewash by herb doctors. If your eyes are red, you can use the over-the-counter remedy, Murine, or opt for your own home remedy, aloe tea. Naturally, if your eyes don't lose their bloodshot look, consult your doctor about what is wrong with them. It could be infection, so be very careful about how you treat your eyes.

Camphor

Camphor oil is what our grandmothers used on earaches, and so it remains if herbal remedies are used around the house. Today, however, the nature of earaches in children has changed as I listen to mothers say that their youngsters had ear infections that only a doctor could treat. What used to be a matter of concern for mothers when their children got earaches has turned into a major worry. I don't know of one mother who wouldn't take her child immediately to the obstetrician if an earache appeared. But if you're positive it's not an infection, then you might try the camphor oil routine.

Onion

Here's a new one on most of us! Onion is very good to take when you have a sore throat—the kind leading to a cold and not a variety of more serious diseases such as tonsillitis, etc. Peel an onion and chew away. There is no warning about eating too much of it, but I would think that as much as you can stand is a good dose. No, really, just a few slices should be taken at any given time, and its juice will soothe your sore throat.

Rue

Here is a home remedy used in the Southwest, especially around Texas by Mexican-Americans. Take rue, make it into an emulsion in lard, and then use it to stop earaches by putting some inside the ear. This remedy is strictly a "no-no" for pregnant women, and low doses of the rue remedy are recommended in any case. You may want to check with your herb doctor to see what he has to say about the poisonous aspects of this remedy.

NERVOUS SYSTEM

Orange

This provides a remedy that can be used only if you have access to an orange tree. All parts of the orange and tree including the flowers are to be used as an infusion, decoction, tincture, or syrup to treat insomnia and to soothe one's nerves. A friend of mine who has a mother in her late seventies living in the country talks about her nerves. She sees a foreign-born doctor who really isn't familiar with aging farm women who complain about their nerves. But nerves are nerves and the way to treat them is with orange decoction—pills just won't do. This woman has been taking pills of every variety her doctor can try on her and none of them has done a thing for her nerves. My friend hasn't tried the orange cure on her yet, but soon will to delay Mother's fears and complaints. I'm surprised she doesn't know the cure herself because many rural people early on learn about home remedies and what to take for what ailment.

VITAMINS

Many of the herbal remedies are high in vitamin content and can be taken just for that reason. Alfalfa, which you might take in the morning, is high in Vitamins K, D, A, E, C, and B complex. So you can make some alfalfa tea and have all of your vitamins, too. What you want to check with your herb doctor is how much alfalfa you need to take to get the recommended daily amount of the vitamin into your system. The same is true for the other herbs. Determine the dosage you should use for yourself. Rosehip in fruit, soup, or jam form, is high in vitamin C and vitamin A. Cayenne (red pepper) is, in infusion form, high in vitamin A. Oranges, which most people usually drink as juice in the morning, are high in vitamin C, and also can be taken as an infusion, decoction, tincture, and syrup. So you can prepare your vitamins in advance and have them on hand for the mornings when you take them.

IV

More Teas and Herbal Remedies

Althea Root

This root is recommended as a mouthwash, and as a douche. If taken internally under doctor's care, it has the effect of easing the throat and lungs and soothing them. But if it's a douche, too, you may be sure that it's powerful and one of those herbs that you really don't want to experiment with on yourself. You need to let the herb doctor know you're going to try this herb and get his recommendation about appropriate dosage for your system. Mine is that you don't take much of this, and use it externally and internally only with an herb doctor's say-so.

Bayberry Bark

Bayberry is effective in bleeding and is good to use as a gargle as well. If you have bleeding gums, use bayberry bark before you get to the dentist, and if you have, say, a bloody nose, bayberry bark should stop it. Don't ever let your gums go as I did one time when I had gingevitis and the dentist scraped away the rotting tissue around every tooth in my mouth. Since that time, I've taken very good care of my teeth because I have no intention of going through that terrible pain again. It's much worse than root canal work, which I've had my share of, and I'm convinced that you should be careful to treat your gums with respect.

Bearberry

This herb is not only good for the kidneys, but also helps reduce uric acid in the system. This would be an especially effective herbal remedial tea for those suffering with gout. Check with your herb doctor to make certain you should take this tea if you're having gout or kidney difficulties, and with his permission, go ahead with treating yourself with this tea.

Black Cohosh Root

This root, made into a tea, is good for relaxing your nerves, stress, pre-menstrual syndrome, menopause, and childbirth pains. You don't want to take it while pregnant, but it can be an effective painkiller during childbirth. If you're planning a natural childbirth, then black cohosh may be good for you to take if the pain turns really bad. But you'd need to be having the baby at home assisted by a midwife or an herbal doctor who would allow the use of this remedy.

Blueberry

Now here's a home remedy that has been supplanted by modern medicine. This plant's leaf is good for regulating blood sugar in minor diabetes and hypoglycemia. This dangerous set of conditions should be treated by a physician, but if he knows about the efficacy of blueberry leaf, then tell him about it and that you'd like to try it. If he says it's okay, then try what the herbal doctor recommends. You will have to consult him to find out just what dosage you need to treat your ailment. Please be very careful about treating yourself with herbs when attempting to combat a serious illness.

Boneset

This tea has two healers in the same infusion. If you drink the tea hot, then it's good for helping to break flu and fevers. But as a cool, perhaps iced tea, remedy, it's good for use as a laxative. So it seems to be a sound idea to have some boneset tea around to use as a remedy for what ails you.

Burdock Leaves

I have a friend who recently got poison ivy all over his arms and legs while he was digging up weeds in the backyard. While he went to his doctor, nothing much was recommended to care for the condition. When it comes to poison ivy, I feel that home remedies are just as strong and effective as modern medications. Take leaves of the burdock and dampen them to put around infected areas. Leave them on till it's clear the condition is healing up. If you find that it isn't working well, then check with your physician.

Calendula

This is marigold, too, and it's good for aiding your digestion, ulcers, and stomach cramps. It is also excellent for external use on bruises and boils. If you have ulcers, you naturally want to know what is the best way to treat them, and your herb doctor may have more remedies to suggest. Your physician will recommend a medication that is helping to make ulcers a common ailment that can be treated. You seldom hear anymore of ulcers as being life-threatening because of drugs that keep them from growing worse and letting them heal naturally. But if you have other minor stomach symptoms that you know about and want to treat with calendula, then go ahead. It's best to check with an herb doctor on amounts to use for treating these ailments.

Cascara Bark

This tea is made from cascara bark and available where herbal teas are sold is a well-known and effective laxative. Head straight for a cascara bark tea if you begin to suffer constipation that you know is caused by your diet. If the constipation lasts through the tea, you should call your physician. Anything that approaches a week with no bowel movement should be serious and in need of medical assistance. Before letting the condition go on too long, see if the cascara bark tea won't loosen your bowels when you first realize you're constipated.

Chickweed

If taken internally, chickweed helps kill bronchitis. And if you take it externally as a poultice, it will heal boils. It's always good to know what is causing your boils so I wouldn't just merrily go about treating them without finding out first what's causing them. Boils don't seem to be as prevalent today as they once were. They've gone the way of the ulcer. But if you get one, treat it with chickweed poultices and make an appointment with your doctor.

Coltsfoot

Coltsfoot tea is just the thing to take to break up colds when they're in your chest and in combination with appropriate medicine if you have bronchitis. But it is mainly used as an expectorant when you need to cough up the phlegm associated with colds and bronchitis. It's good for asthma, too, so you might consult your herbal doctor to see if he recommends the use of coltsfoot with whatever ailment you have.

Comfrey Leaf

Use this herb, mixing it with Vaseline, on wounds, rashes, and burns. Naturally, if the problem is severe, you should go to the hospital. But if you just slightly burn yourself on the stove or cut yourself with a kitchen knife, then comfrey is fine.

Comfrey Root

Before we had the comfrey leaf, and now we have the root. This remedy is good for encouraging the speedy recovery of cells and on other internal irritations and helps heal broken bones. If you're in a hospital nursing a broken leg, you will not be given comfrey root to speed your recovery. But if you are at home and the break isn't that serious, or is well on its way to mending, you might add comfrey root to your diet. Ask your herb doctor if he recommends it. He may have another altogether different herb to take, but this is a first-class one so he may give you the go-ahead.

Damiana

This is a true aphrodisiac and it stimulates your sexual drive. When taken internally, it is known to also bring into balance any hormonal difficulties you may be having. You can't lose using this as an aphrodisiac, but because it is so powerful, you should consult your herb doctor to find out how much to take.

Devil's Claw

The devil's claw is an anti-inflammatory to help relieve arthritis and rheumatism. I've been using it to treat tendinitis in my feet, and it seems to help. I am to be given medication for my ailment soon, another anti-inflammatory in pill form, but if the devil's claw brings more relief, then I shall start taking it again.

Eucalyptus Leaf

Make a tea of this and inhale it as a treatment for asthma, stuffy noses, and coughs. It can also be combined with oil and put on your skin as an insect repellent. But it works best on colds. Take the tea too to aid in the healing process (although check with your doctor about this approach because eucalyptus is primarily a medication that you use externally).

Eyebright

This herb is the best one for protecting the health of eyes. If you're prone to eye weakness, cysts, and conjunctivitis, then you should find out from your herb doctor if he recommends the use of eyebright to alleviate these conditions. The eyes are such a sensitive organ you don't want to overuse an herb to the point of danger. Therefore, to avoid harming your eyes, you should take the best advice as to using a powerful herbal drug such as eyebright.

Fenugreek Seed

This herb has to be taken internally as a tea to be used against bronchitis and fevers. When I see one of these remedies for bronchitis, I always advise that you should stick closely to what your physician recommends. Bronchitis can quickly turn to pneumonia which can be dangerous and difficult to get rid of. Take care of yourself and follow doctor's orders.

Hawthorn Berries

As a tea, hawthorn berries are extremely helpful in aiding the heart if there are ailments in attendance. They also help to regulate blood pressure. If your herb doctor thinks that the hawthorn berries in tea form are likely to help you with severe conditions involving the heart and blood pressure, then you may go ahead and use this remedy. But, as in all situations where there's an important organ of the body involved, you should first get the opinion of a professional who should know if it's right for you to use the remedy.

Hops

Since hops are used in beer making, it isn't surprising that they would be just the thing to relax you. Hops made into a tea have a calming effect and recommended for diarrhea when brought on by nerves. It's also a good tea to make and take if you are restless or have insomnia. You don't need much to make a tea, and its effect should be soporific to your system.

Horehound

This is an excellent remedy to use when you need an expectorant. It's effective for coughs and bronchitis, and you can take it as a tea or as horehound candy which you often find sold generally. Horehound is probably very effective on coughs, but, as always with bronchitis, I'd check with a doctor before treating myself with home remedies.

Juniper Berries

These are holistic in nature, too, and should be used as a digestive aid and tonic for the stomach. It helps ease coughs and would be very good with smoker's hack. So if you easily get upset stomachs (maybe as a hangover), try juniper berries made into a tea and see if you don't feel better fast.

Licorice Root

By now, you're getting quite a medicine chest full of antidotes to bronchitis. I can't stress strongly enough that you need to consult with a doctor to see if it's okay to take these medications in combination with his diagnosed prescription. Licorice root is good for healing tissues that have become inflamed with the disease, and helps with coughs and congestion.

Linden Flowers

This is an antispasmodic and is good for flu, colds, and sore throats. Since there really aren't any better medications on the market, you might as well go with linden flowers. And if you apply them on acne, it should help with that, too. It's also good for burns, but you want to be sure which ones to treat with the flowers. Bad burns should be examined by your doctor, and you shouldn't treat them (except perhaps with ice water) till you see him and find out just how serious they are.

Mullein Leaf

This herb is good for coughs and bronchitis. If externally applied, it will help reduce swelling of the glands in the neck, piles, and skin wounds if they're not serious. Make sure the leaves are wet before you apply them, and let them dry on the area you're treating. You may wish to lay some on your chest if you have coughs or bronchitis that can be treated this way. Make sure what the cough is and check with your doctor to see if you can use the remedy in conjunction with his prescribed medication.

Myrrh Gum

This herb is extremely helpful with teeth and gums when you begin to suffer from pyorrhea. And, indeed, you can use it on sores on your skin. If you have a bedridden person who has bedsores, this myrrh gum is an effective remedy for them. Ask your dentist about using myrrh gum on your teeth to see if there is something else you should be taking with it. To strengthen gums, he sometimes prescribes hydrogen peroxide that's used on the hair, so I can't see the harm in using myrrh gum, which I understand is a fine healing remedy.

Nettle Leaf

This stimulates the digestive system, and is also supposed to be good for nursing mothers to increase their milk output (check with an herbal doctor on this before using while pregnant). It also makes a wonderful hair tonic and hair rinse (see the necessity for asking the herbal doctor. What you use externally should not be powerful enough to frighten you when you go to take the remedy internally.) The doctor will probably say please stick to the hair rinse, and I would agree.

Peppermint

Here is a well-known remedy, as grandmothers often gave out oil of peppermint to youngsters for upset stomachs and the like. Peppermint tea also is recommended for flatulence and nausea, so if you have either ailment, sip away. It is said that it improves the digestion, so have a tea or two during the day to make you feel really well.

Psyllium Husk

Here's one for the digestive tract that I think is probably a good home remedy. It has natural bulk and helps keep the intestinal tract moving along with regularity. Carbohydrates are slowed by the psyllium from being absorbed and thus your blood sugar is controlled to some degree. If you want to use it for this purpose, I'd check with my herb doctor as to the proper dosage. But I think any medication that treats the intestines with bulk to keep them moving and healthy is a worthy one to try.

Red Clover

Red clover is also helpful in treating the immune system and purifies the blood (and we all need it purified now and then). It is also soothing to the bronchial passages and might be just the medication to have on hand when you first catch cold. You might be able to keep your bronchial passages free of the disease if you start early treatment of it.

Red Raspberry

This plant is especially good for strengthening the female organs during pregnancy. It eases childbirth, prevents miscarriage, and increases milk. I would check with the herb doctor to see if the dosage is right for you, especially if you're pregnant, and he may recommend leaving your system alone as much as possible. I know I certainly would recommend that, and add that in this condition you should stop smoking and drinking alcohol of any kind as well as taking drugs. Adding anything foreign or addictive to the system is bad for the unborn baby. So if you're planning to use some raspberry, check to make sure that you should.

Sarsaparilla

Here's yet another use of this home remedy. It is good both for male impotence and for the defense mechanisms of the body. I should think that an AIDS patient might take sarsaparilla without too much worry, as there is no proven cure for the disease as yet. The only thing you might want to know from a physician is if it would interfere with AZT or whatever the AIDS patient is taking to strengthen the immune system.

Sassafras Leaf

Sassafras has been mentioned in this book before, but I have another use for it: for blemishes on the face. If you're an adolescent, this will be especially helpful, and if you're an adult with oily skin that still breaks out just as it did when you were a teenager, then you'll be happy to know about this tea, too. Another use of sassafras is as a blood purifier, so if you're into cleaning your blood now and then, this is the right medication. Vegetarians, I know, are interested in purifying their blood, and we all should be open to treating ourselves now and then with a tonic for the system.

Saw Palmetto Berry

As a tea, this turns out to be an amazing aphrodisiac. It's supposed to increase sexual appetite dramatically. So, if you're into trying new herbs for sexual stimulation, you won't be disappointed with this one. You might ask the herb doctor more about it before experimenting, such as the dosage to use. You may be able to get saw palmetto from an herb shop and it can help with the dosage. But it certainly is worth trying if you need this kind of stimulation.

Senna Leaf

This is a powerful laxative which is recommended for severe cases of constipation. It cleanses the bowel, and turns the user into a happy camper again. It is often used for chronic constipation, so you should consult the herb specialist about how much to take in order to get the desired effects.

Slippery Elm Bark

This remedy falls into the holistic health way to treat your body. It soothes and heals mucous membranes in the lungs, throat, and vagina. So if you feel like your organs are drying (which they probably are with age) then once in a while have some slippery elm bark as a tea.

Skullcap

This herb is used to fix all kinds of problems with the nervous system. It's effective for hysteria, convulsions, and tremors. It quiets the restless soul and relieves insomnia. Hysteria is a very real and threatening disorder that needs psychiatric attention. If you can't readily get to a psychiatrist, however, you could try using skullcap in the interim. There are so many modern wonder drugs for psychiatric conditions that hysteria is probably treatable with one of them. After all, if schizophrenia and manic depression, two of the more serious diseases that one can get in the mental area, are treatable and people are able to go back to work and have a normal life while taking the medication, then hysteria must be treatable, too. Convulsions and tremors, as far as I'm concerned, should always be treated by a physician, who must find out what's causing them and then treat accordingly. It just isn't a good idea to treat them with home remedies.

Watermelon Seed

Here is an interesting bit of lore about those annoying watermelon seeds. They're a diuretic, and some people take them successfully to regulate high blood pressure. You might as well try it because all of the diuretics that are offered for the condition today have drawbacks of one sort or another. Ask your herb doctor about this, then go ahead and try it. I don't know of any side effects from the seed, but you'll want to be sure you have the right dosage before using it on high blood pressure.

Witch Hazel Leaf

There are a number of uses for the witch hazel leaf. If you take it as a tea, it's good for nerves and diarrhea. If you use the leaf externally, it will serve well as a gargle and even a vaginal douche. Anything you can gargle with and also use as a douche needs, it seems to me, to be checked out with an herb doctor. I think I would like to get the proper dosage before trying it.

Yellow Dock Root

This is a blood purifier that can also be used externally for eruptions on the skin (such as pimples) and for itches and rashes. Make a poultice of the yellow dock root for your face and put it on the areas where the pimples and blemishes have erupted. Leave till dry and it will easily come off. If you have a rash that doesn't seem to be a complex symptom of another disease, you may use it as a poultice on the rash.

FOR DIETING PEOPLE

The herbal teas which follow are good for ridding the body of excess fat, therefore helping you on your way to losing weight.

Bladderwrack

This herb, which contains a lot of natural iodine, is also believed to be good for reducing cellulite deposits, although I look at the effectiveness of bladderwrack with a skeptical eye. So far, the only remedies that anyone believes remove cellulite appear in advertisements on television and in the back of fashion magazines. You might want to try bladderwrack if all else has failed to remove your cellulite. But I wouldn't bet this cure-all remedy is any better than what's advertised elsewhere.

Chickweed

This is a diuretic and it helps keep you away from the refrigerator between meals. You should probably not take more than two teas a day of the chickweed, and your diet should be well-balanced with fewer calories and a lot of exercise to bring off the pounds.

Fennel

This remedy soothes the stomach while on a diet. You could make a tea of fennel to dull the effects of appetite on the stomach. It tends to go to fatty deposits and helps get rid of them. Fennel, which has been around for a very long time, is one of the major dietary herbs.

Hawthorn Berries

Here is another herb with claims that may or may not be true. It is said to remove fatty deposits and cholesterol in the blood. If it can do these things, then more power to it. But I'd ask an herb doctor what he thinks of the effectiveness of hawthorn berries on these particular fat issues.

Licorice Root

Here's something I didn't say about licorice root earlier: it is effective in stopping your craving for sugar. It has natural sweetness and while you're controlling your sugar cravings, you are, at the same time, stimulating your liver to cleanse the body of excess fat. Licorice may very well be the home remedy that can do this, and if the herb doctor agrees, go ahead and try to get your liver to cleanse your body.

Sarsaparilla

Again, sarsaparilla shows up as a powerful body cleanser and blood purifier. It is a source of plant hormones that stimulate the glands to rid the body of fatty poisons. Since I've put on some weight in recent years, I'm going to try sarsaparilla as a cleanser before getting into my diet-exercise routine.

V

Unusual Home Remedies

Apple Tree

A tea made of the bark of the apple tree is excellent for flavor, suppressed menstruation, nausea, vomiting, and low fever. All you need do is take several cups of the tea and you should begin to feel better. As I often advise, see a physician if you have symptoms like these I've mentioned, as they may mean you're really sick with something else.

Balomy

This is a good remedy for eczema, which a friend of mine had when she was a little girl. It's very itchy and a miserable condition to have. Use balomy for it if you've tried everything else. This herb also stimulates the appetite, so if you've a bad cold and don't want to eat, have some balomy to restore your appetite.

Bay Leaves

Make a tea of bay leaves, and you will find that they're good for letting wind from your bowels as well as being effective for cramps. If you don't need to take bay leaves for these problems, it's still a fine tonic for the stomach. If you just want to make your stomach feel better, bay leaf is just the ticket.

Beech Bark and Leaves

If you're lucky enough to have a beech tree by your house, then take some of the bark and leaves and make a tea of them. If there's no tree nearby, the herbalist may have some. The bark and leaves are good for ulcers, internal and external. If you have ulcers on your legs, use a poultice of the leaves. It's also a sound idea to take the beech as a tonic once in a while to help rid your system of poisons that may have accumulated.

Beetroot

This is an all-around remedy for things of the uterus that ail you. It's even good for a fallen womb for which you should go to the doctor. Mine has been reset as it got out of place and it's a procedure that only takes a minute. Beetroot is also a good remedy for common diarrhea, and is effective for coughs and lung conditions. You might want to try it on smoker's cough to see if that doesn't clear up.

Bistort Root

This makes an excellent remedy for sore gums. If mixed with equal parts of raspberry, it's good on cankers that are internal in nature. Before going through all this, ask your herb doctor about dosage. If you're combining two herb remedies, you need to know the exact amount to take of each. This is an old-fashioned remedy and is therefore good for sting, insect bites, snake bites, and for expelling worms. If bitten by a poisonous snake, you should of course get medical attention right away. But if the common garter snake bit you, then you're okay taking some bistort root.

Blue Violet

The claims for this plant go all the way to curing cancer. I certainly doubt it, but if you have cancer and it's being treated medically, ask if you can try the blue violet, too. It's good for bringing comfort to internal ulcers, so you might try it on that condition.

Bloodroot

This remedy is good for a variety of ailments among which are sore throat and syphillitic problems. It's effective on bronchitis, laryngitis, and pneumonia, as well as some skin diseases. Small doses of bloodroot stimulate the digestive system, and large doses act as a sedative. You need to consult your herbal doctor about what kind of dosage you need for which problem. As far as being good for syphillis, I would see a physician immediately. If the herb doctor says you can combine it with antibiotics to no ill effect, then you may take some bloodroot too.

Broom

This makes an excellent ointment for dealing with lice or other vermin that get in your hair. It's also good for everything from ague to gout, and in combination with dandelion, it cleans out your kidneys and bladder. You should treat the gout very carefully and take whatever modern medications are good for it, but you may also be able to take broom if you get permission from your herb doctor.

Buckbean

This plant is good for getting rid of worms, and it promotes a fine digestive system by increasing gastric juices. It's effective for jaundice as well as liver and kidney troubles, and even helps rheumatism as well as some fevers. You need to consult about dosage.

Buckthorn Bark

This plant keeps the bowels on a regular schedule and is good for constipation. It is also effective for skin diseases. Drinking a hot cup will produce a lot of perspiration, and as an ointment, it cures itchy patches of skin. Another remedial property of buckthorn bark may be for warts. As we grow older, more and more warts start to appear, and the buckthorn bark is just the thing to combat these.

Burnet

Drinking one or more cold cups of this root during the day provides the best relief known for stomach ailments. It cleanses the stomach and makes it feel better right away. So if you feel nauseous after a heavy meal, or if your stomach is in bad condition because you drank too much the night before, try burnet root and you'll feel better fast. If used externally, it is good for cuts and earache, applied as a poultice.

Calamus Root

Taken internally, calamus is especially good for the stomach. If you don't want to take Alka Seltzer or any of the other over-the-counter remedies for upset stomachs, then try calamus for the same effect. Another use is as a destroyer of the desire for tobacco. Instead of "cold turkeying" cigarettes, try calamus root for a few weeks as a tea and you should lose your desire for cigarettes. If the Nicorette chewing gum doesn't work for you, perhaps this remedy will. The calamus tea is also good externally as a poultice for burns and sores.

Just wash with the tea, and the condition should heal up in several days.

Cascara Sagrada

This plant is best known for being effective for constipation, as an all-around good intestinal medication, and it has been used as well for gallstone removal and liver complaints. Drink one or two cups a day of the tea made from it, and you'll feel much more like yourself. This bark made into pills can be found in some pharmacies and health food stores, and should be kept on hand so that when your stomach turns sour, you can immediately take one and feel better fast.

Cedron

This is one of those country remedies for poisonous insect and snakebites. You make a tea of the cedron and put it on a cloth over the bite. Keep it wet and also drink some of the tea as you do this. It is said to work well, but I know that if I had a poisonous bite, I'd immediately go to the local clinic or hospital for treatment. So if you don't live where such a facility is convenient, and are in a rural area, then cedron is what you need as you seek medical assistance.

Chickweed

Gardeners will be amazed that this common weed is good for anything. It in fact can be used fresh or as a salve and poultice or fomentation, and is effective for colds, coughs, bronchitis, as well as the bowels and stomach. It's especially good for inflammations of any kind as well as simple burns and skin diseases. Make a poultice for the external ailments until swelling goes down. You should, of course, not substitute medical help for any unusual conditions or ailments, but to keep things under control, by all means use chickweed.

Chicory

This is a famous additive to coffee in the South. It is also a home remedy and is especially good for upset stomachs. You need to be ready for the kind of cure chicory effects on upset stomachs, as it brings up the offending gastrointestinal material, and doesn't just soothe it. I'll stick with my Alka Seltzer, thank you, but if you've swallowed something that should come up, then bet on chicory to do the job. Chicory is also good for the kidneys and urinary tract, and acts as a laxative and diuretic. This is a handy and easy-to-find remedy to keep around the house for sudden ill conditions.

Cleavers

Cleavers has been mentioned and makes a wonderful face wash for those with pimples. It helps clear the face up in no time and should work well on adolescents with acne. Some claim cleavers to be good for skin cancer, but I certainly wouldn't want to rely on it if that was my condition and would immediately consult my physician. Cleavers is also good for eczema, and you might try it for that. If you serve the plant as you would spinach, it makes a wonderful blood cleansing agent.

Columbo

This is a tropical remedy that acts as a tonic for the entire system, and is good for fevers too. It is especially effective 'n hot humid places, and is recommended to combat dysentery and cholera. I would guess that if you're a long way from the doctors, you might try columbo for these ailments as a stop-gap measure. But for diseases like cholera and dysentery, you really need the proper modern medication to stamp it out of your system.

Coral Root

This is a powerful remedy for skin diseases, effective for scrofula, scurvy, oils, tumors, and night sweats among others. It's also highly recommended for cancer. If your doctor is the try-anything type in the area of advanced cancer, then coral root is something you should try. Also, make a tea and use poultices on boils and tumors of all kinds. Again, you need to see a physician to tell you why you have these skin eruptions.

Cubeb Berries

This is an excellent remedy for chronic bladder problems. It's generally used in cooking but the cubeb pepper's claimed to help cure low fevers and is effective for menstruation cramps. It is also said to be good for typhus, but if you have it, you need a doctor, so I wouldn't try it to see if it heals the condition. But if you're out in the countryside or the jungle and need a fast temporary remedy for typhus, then by all means try cubeb berries.

Dill

You'll be happy to hear that dill provides just the remedy if you have the hiccoughs. If your hiccoughing is prolonged, then try dill to see if it works wonders. It's also good for general pains and swelling if you've twisted your arm or leg. It's excellent for combatting nervousness, and might be the right remedy if you must make a public performance of some kind. Just take some dill and you'll feel calm before you go on stage. This dill, incidentally, is the same herb used to make dill pickles. So it's nice to know that your cooking herb is also a healing one.

Echinacea

This is known as an excellent blood cleanser and has been used throughout the years for some very serious conditions, such as gangrene, peritonitis, diphteria, and tonsillitus, to name a few. But I recommend it for a scratchy throat for which you need a gargle, and also for sores or perhaps infections. I think that I am right in warning you about the diseases and conditions that are recommended by herbalists for echinacea, as modern medicine can cure them much better than the herbs can. I certainly wouldn't want peritonitis treated just with an herb when it may require an operation. Some of the ailments for which this herb is said to be effective are life and death ones, and I'm very hesitant to recommend any herb under those conditions.

Elecampane

This plant I recommend for bronchitis (in addition to modern medication), bad coughs, and colds. It has other uses, but bronchitis is a serious enough disease to mention as being healed by this herb. If you want to ask your herb doctor what he suggests elecampane for, go right ahead, but I'm not going to recommend that a serious illness be treated with herbs.

Fit Root

Here we have a root that is good for calming the nerves and the condition of feeling faint. It does, as most of the herbs I've talked about, have other uses, but I'm not impressed. Fit root is thought to be a cure for lockjaw. I doubt that very much and warn you that the lockjaw will lead to death and should not be treated by medicinal herbs.

Gentian Root

As a tonic, it's a blood purifier, and it's effective with liver problems. It improves your appetite if you've been feeling wan, and it's also an excellent remedy for colds and fever. If you urine isn't hearty, it's good for that, too. And, if you happen to get a snakebite or a bite from a poisonous bug, gentian root is just the remedy until you can see a doctor.

Gold Thread Root

This root is very good when you have ulcers or even canker sores in your mouth. It is supposed to keep you from craving alcohol and I have a number of imbibing friends I've told about this cure. They haven't reported back to me yet on the root's effectiveness, but I would at least recommend trying it for alcohol addiction as there are no easy modern cures for the disease.

Holy Thistle

This plant is effective for strengthening memory. Although it's also good for the liver and lungs, the memory problems are the ones I'm most interested in with holy thistle. It's also effective for insanity, but which kind I'm not certain. I can't think that holy thistle would be effective on such dire conditions as schizophrenia or manic depression, but if you've tried the modern medications and they don't work, you might be tempted to experiment with holy thistle.

Indian Hemp

Hemp, of course, is used to make rope, but the root makes a fine home remedy. It's good for colds and the flu, and since it causes a flood of perspiration, is effective for helping break up fevers. Hemp has been used in treating diabetes or even mumps. For mumps, you brew a tea of the root and have several cups during the day, and at the same time you can make a poultice of it and put in on the bumps caused by the mumps. Another condition for which hemp is good is hiccoughs. If you've tried putting your head in a paper bag and it hasn't cured your hiccoughs, or taken some bitters and lemon, then go with some hemp tea and maybe you'll get relief.

Lungwort

This plant (all of it usable) is especially good with coughs and the flu. Get a supply of lungwort to have on hand during the flu season. Among the other conditions for which it's also recommended are yellow jaundice and lung trouble of every kind (including bleeding lungs), things I'd personally go to the doctor to have treated. I really don't think you should try to treat such serious ailments with plant remedies when the doctor will treat you as if you're very ill and need modern medication. But for colds or the flu, lungwort is a very strong plant to use, and I'd keep it on hand for those.

Magnolia Bark

This remedy is good for combatting fevers and has been used for dysentery, among other diseases. It is also effective in getting rid of smoking. You take this and the desire fades for a cigarette. Magnolia bark can be used in place of quinine, but I certainly wouldn't change my doctor's prescription of that drug without getting his advice.

Masterwort

Masterwort is effective for colds and fevers, and for suppressing menstruation. It's also used for epilepsy. Again, I warn that you wouldn't want to override the advice of a doctor in the treatment of epilepsy, but if you want to take it because of gas, go ahead.

Marshmallow

In a liquid form of the root, this is an excellent diuretic, and as a poultice, it can be used for sore spots and even to bathe sore eyes as it's a very soothing herbal remedy. If you have hoarseness, gargle with it, and it can be used as a douche for minor irritation of the female parts. It's a fine remedy for pneumonia if you can't reach a physician right away to treat you.

Milkweed

Milkweed, which is the lovely herb that has silk attached to the seeds, is very good for increasing the flow of urine and for easing female complaints, such as vaginal itch. Again, see a gynecologist if the itch doesn't immediately disappear. It's also effective for asthma and is generally good for liver complaints. Make into a tea and have two cups daily.

Mint

We all probably have had mint juleps occasionally or other drinks using this aromatic plant, so it's a surprise to find mint on the list of home remedies. But the mint plant (make a tea) is good for soothing pain. If your feet hurt after a long day on them, then have a cup of mint tea and they'll feel better before long. Also, if your menstrual flow isn't strong, take mint to strengthen it. And if you suffer from nausea, then try some mint to try to keep the condition at bay. Be careful, however, if you frequently have nausea for unexplained reasons. Sometimes it can be a warning signal for other dangerous illnesses. And if you are suffering from a gassy stomach, mint will take care of that effectively. My advice is to keep a supply on hand to ease what ails you.

Motherwort

Motherwort is a plant that is good for treating such conditions as hysteria and nervousness of any kind. The plant is also useful when treating menstrual cramps. A fomentation of hot tea takes care of the condition. This is a good remedy for young women to have on hand whose cramps are severe and haven't cleared up with more modern medicines. Sometimes home remedies are the better choice for certain conditions.

Origanum

Origanum, also known as wild marjoram, is useful for treating a poor stomach, and increasing appetite. It's also effective for a bad cough, especially if you're been smoking too much. This plant is good, too, as an eardrop for clearing up problems such as earwax. Origanum is effective, in addition, for a gassy stomach and, as a poultice, it's good for sprains and boils, and even for nervous conditions.

Peach

The marvelous peach tree, which provides home remedies with bark, leaves, twigs, and kernels, should be in every yard. The leaves, boiled into a tea, make an excellent laxative, and they're also good for nerves. Peach is said to be quite effective in the remedying of whooping cough but I don't recommend it for that. See instead what the doctor prescribes for this nasty childhood disease. You don't want to take a chance with a child's health. The leaves, when made into tea, are said to be good for combatting morning sickness if you're pregnant. I would guess that it's alright to take a few swallows of tea if you have the morning sickness, but watch your intake and speak to an herb doctor before treating yourself with your condition if you're the slightest bit nervous.

Pennyroyal

Pennyroyal is excellent if you have a high fever. It promotes perspiration to break up the fever, and should be taken hot. It's also a very good remedy for toothache, colds, phlegm that comes from a cold in your chest, cramps, headaches, and ulcers. If you have ulcers, though, check with your physician. Home remedies are no longer useful if modern medicine comes up with something better.

Plantain

Again, I am just delighted that the plantain, which is found in tropical places, is a home remedy as it's a wonderful dish (try fried plantain sometime). Its leaves are good used as a remedy for wounds. As paste, made by pounding the plantain leaves, it is just the thing to put on a wound that doesn't need stitches, and also is effective on burns and as a remedy for eczema. Use the paste or make a tea of the leaves and apply it to the burns.

Pleurisy Root

Besides being a very good remedy for pleurisy, this plant can be used for breaking up colds or flu and combatting bronchial problems. It's good with most severe fevers coming from such diseases as scarlet fever, typhus, and measles, and for asthma as well. If you have pleurisy, you may call a herb doctor to get the correct remedy for it, or you should see a physician. So many of these home remedies at one time provided the only cure for a variety of diseases, but now they've been replaced with modern medicines that may or may not be as effective. You need to check for yourself what you take. Often there is a doctor-prescribed medication that is better than a home remedy for the condition you have. But home remedies do work, as they have for generations, so they can't be just cast aside. It would be foolhardy to do so when many diseases are treated more effectively with herbs than newer medication.

Psylla

This plant is a fine assistant remedy (see the doctor for modern cure) in such conditions as ulcer and hemorrhoids. It's also an excellent cleanser of the intestines and helps prevent diverticulitis. Take a spoonful with your food, or, if you wish, in a glass of hot water about an hour before dinner.

Quassia

The wood and bark of the quassia is a strong remedy for getting rid of the compulsion to drink. So you can see that even in early times people had a problem with alcohol and tried to do something about it, and if it worked then, it probably works now. The only contemporary remedy that seems to have a lasting effect on alcoholism is a lifelong membership in AA, which brings together recovering alcoholics to share their experience, strength and hope. Quassia is also good for combatting fevers and rheumatism. In fact, if someone in the house drinks, have the wood and bark of the quassia around for emergencies.

Queen of the Meadow

This lovely sounding remedy is good for the bladder, chronic urinary problems, and neuralgia, as well as for rheumatism and for relaxing the nerves. Since it increases the flow of urine, it is so good with problems in this area, and should be kept on hand at all times. If your symptoms don't indicate a trip to the doctor, then try some queen of the meadow for your home cure.

Ragwort

Ragwort is definitely a woman's plant, whose parts are used to cure various female complaints. It can be used for curing leukorrhea (a white discharge from the vagina) and also for cases where menstruation is suppressed or not on schedule. Ragwort is good for all cases of urinary disease, although you will want to check with your herb doctor to see how he prescribes it.

Red Clover

Once again, here's a plant whose flower is the healer. Some people have used it to good effect in destroying cancer cells. To help ease the condition, take teas of the flower and it will calm nerves, cure bronchial problems and make a healing salve when added to Vaseline.

Red Root

This is a remedy for spleen problems. Take it as a tonic for these troubles and perhaps you won't have to undergo an operation to have the spleen removed. Red root, using the root parts, is also good for bronchitis and asthma, and as a great mouthwash if you have cankers or a sore mouth that needs attending to. In addition, it can reduce the swelling to tonsils that haven't been removed. You roll it around in your mouth as a strong tea every few hours if you have tonsil problems. It's also an effective treatment for hemorrhoids. Ask your herb doctor about red root before treating yourself, however, especially if you have spleen or tonsil problems.

Rock Rose

Rock rose is good for combatting diarrhea, and infections such as syphillis and gonorrhea. If you do decide to treat yourself this way, get a doctor's opinion. Penicillin is a remedy that's usually effective. You don't want the condition to become worse while you try out various remedies. It's also said that rock rose is good as a remedy for cancer. If you're a terminal case then it wouldn't hurt to experiment with the rock rose cure, but I wouldn't use it while the cancer is in early stages and possibly can be cured with modern medicines.

Sanicle

This plant (root and leaves) is used for everything you can imagine as it's an old remedy and is a cure-all. Put a heaping teaspoonful of the sanicle in a cup of water. Let it steep for half an hour, then drink five or six cups a day. It's good for bowel problems, and will stop whatever pain might accompany it. If you have pain in your bowels, you obviously should consult a doctor. Again, sanicle is good for the sexual diseases, and is used also to clear the body of poisons. As a gargle, it's fine for ridding the mouth and stomach of mucous.

Saw Palmetto Berries

Again, fresh or dried berries of the saw palmetto in a tea make an excellent remedy for asthma and sore throats. It's especially good with colds, and helps with bronchitis and even whooping cough. You should check with your herb doctor to see if he agrees with saw palmetto berries are what you need with the more dangerous diseases (bronchitis). But for a sore throat, they're fine, as they are with colds. The berries are also good for diabetes, and here you should definitely check an herb doctor to see if he thinks they're all right to use.

Seawrack

This remedy is an excellent weight loss remedy for an overweight person. Three or four cups of hot seawrack tea a day are what's recommended, and you may ask the opinion of an herb doctor to find out if that does it. The seawrack is also good with such disorders as goiter and scrofula. If you have either condition, check with your physician for his recommendations.

Self-Heal

This plant is good for conditions such as epilepsy and even convulsions, and for all kinds of ulcers, like those that you might get around the mouth, or around the vagina. It strikes me that if you have vaginal ulcers, you have some kind of disease and should see a physician. But self-heal is the plant of choice with most ulcers. It may be taken as a tea or as a poultice for external cuts and bruises.

Senna

Senna leaves are the healing parts of the plant and they're best used for bad breath and a sour stomach. Senna also makes an effective laxative, and you should put the leaves in boiling water (one cup) and wait for a while then strain the tea. Drink one cup, or a little more if the first isn't altogether successful. But since it's a laxative, don't drink too much as you'd never get out of the bathroom.

Sorrel

You can eat this plant like a green vegetable, or make a tea from the flowers that is a remedy for ulcers in the stomach. The root is good for heavy flow during menstruation, and is also effective for jaundice. You need medical attention if you have this condition, so don't overlook consulting a physician for that.

Squaw Vine

This plant, as the name indicates, was used by American Indian women to good effect during pregnancy. It is supposed to make childbirth a snap, and is a fine wash for an infant's eyes. If you're going to bathe your infant's eyes, you need to combine the squaw vine with raspberry leaves and witch hazel, or wild strawberry. If you have gonorrhea, get to a doctor, but try this as a stopgap remedy. Squaw vine makes a good potion for female troubles, and you may find it effective for strengthening a weak menstrual flow.

Saint-John's-Wort

This plant is used for uterine problems such as difficulty in urination, diarrhea, dysentery, and other ailments of this type. With dysentery, you need to have the very best medications so also make a trip to your physician. Saint-John's-wort is good for curing irregular menstrual cycles, and for such nervous conditions as hysteria. I once had hysteria and still recall every moment of that pure torture vividly, so I urge you to keep Saint-John's-wort on hand if you're prone to this condition. The doctor wanted to give me a sedative but I refused to take one and just let the hysteria wind down naturally. Don't ever be that foolish; don't live through it if you don't have to. By all means, take a sedative or, if you prefer, a tea of Saint-John's-Wort.

Summer Savory

Here's an aphrodisiac to try if you or your spouse or lover is interested in such potions. It's also a very fine remedy when you catch cold, and if you have a toothache, you can ease the pain with a touch of summer savory. With a toothache, I know from hard experience that a root canal is probably not far behind, so don't even bother doing much for your painful tooth. Just get to the dentist and have the work done on it. It will save a lot of grief from infection if you do have it taken care of right away. In addition to being a home remedy, summer savory is also a cooking herb, and you can use it to good effect in soups and other dishes.

Sweet Balm

Here is an herb that, when taken as hot tea, will ease the pain of menstruation and assorted kidney troubles. If you take sweet balm as a hot tea, it will help colds and flu from making you miserable. It's especially effective in treating nausea and would be a fine "next day" remedy if you had too much to drink. And I recommend it most for alleviating nausea, providing it is caused by something you know about and is not just a symptom for another more serious disorder. When treating conditions, always be aware that they may be the signals for something more serious, so watch them carefully.

Turkey Corn

This is a root (make a tea of it) and is the herb of choice for treating boils. Take the tea and watch them disappear. This herb also has been used to good effect for syphillis, but I certainly wouldn't take it for that purpose. Syphillis must be treated with antibiotics to actually rid the system of the disease. So don't use turkey corn to treat it unless an herb doctor tells you that you can.

Twin Leaf

If you have severe pains, as from arthritis, this herb may be helpful to you. Drink a cupful of the root of this herb and see if your pain comes under control. This is an alternative remedy to drugs (some very highly addictive ones) that are given for pain. If you make a poultice of twin leaf, you can wrap your arthritic joints from the outside and feel the pain disappear.

Uva Ursi

This plant's leaves are said to be very useful in treating such conditions as diabetes and kidney troubles. That's the pronouncement about uva ursi. I, on the other hand, have seen the effects that diabetes has if one doesn't take insulin every day in the right dosage. You would want to consult a physician to see if he agrees that uva ursi is a bona fide remedy for diabetes. It might be useful in kidney disease if not too severe. Uva ursi is another good remedy for piles and hemorrhoids, but should be checked with your herbal doctor to get his approval on using it for these purposes. It's also recommended for gonorrhea, but I say unequivocally that you should see a doctor for that disease and don't fool around with herbs. Venereal disease is very strong and needs a powerful antibiotic to combat it.

Wahoo

Wahoo is effective as a laxative and I think it's a fine idea to try it, as it may be better for your system then some over-the-counter remedies. Take two or three cups a day of tea made of wahoo, as a laxative. It is also used to treat fevers that aren't symptoms of something worse and in need of medical treatment. Take it as a tonic and it will spruce up your system in a big way. I recommend wahoo as a tonic, and you may want to ask your herb doctor just how much to take (how many teas a day) to work effectively. I recommended one tea a day as a tonic (not in combination with others).

Water Pepper

This plant is useful as a remedy not only for weak menstruation but also for coughs and colds. It makes a fine tonic as a tea, and is useful as a poultice for kidney problems. Apply over kidney area and see if it doesn't feel much better. If you have ulcers, take a liquid diet for a few days to go along with a regimen of fruit juice. It's also supposed to act on appendicitis but since you can die from a ruptured organ, I would go immediately to a physician, not an herb doctor, to have it removed surgically.

White Pond Lily

This is a very old home remedy and is especially good when, using the root, made into a douche for female troubles including leukorrhea. It's important to note that this disease has to be cleaned up quickly before it gets in your bloodstream and causes even more serious problems. So if the douching doesn't work in a few days, go to a doctor for a modern remedy. You can take this as a tea as well, as it will be good not only for diarrhea and bowel problems, but also for bronchial problems.

Wild Alum Root

This is the root that, made into a tea, is good for sore gums and bleeding gums after a tooth has been removed. All you need to do is rub some wild alum on the spot and it will stop nosebleeds. If you use powdered alum root on a wound, it will stop the bleeding. If your period is stronger than you like, then make a douche of the root and the bleeding will let up. If you just want a tonic and general healing tea to drink every day, this is the one. Don't keep it up too long, though, without checking your herb doctor. Too much of a good thing often turns against you.

Wild Cherry

Wild cherry is a good system tonic as well as a fine remedy for a bad cold. If you need to get phlegm out of your chest, then take a cup of wild cherry and you'll be able to cough up what ails you. This is supposed to be effective for asthma, but check with the herb doctor to make sure you take the right dosage. And if you have a fever that won't go away, try wild cherry, but if it persists, then see a physician.

Wild Yam

This is what you should take to get a grip on your nerves. If you have a bad day at the office and your boss has yelled at you or otherwise made you uptight, then relax with a cup of tea made with the root of the wild yam. This is recommended, too, for pregnant women. If you take it late in pregnancy, you will find that it soothes you from the burdens you carry.

Wintergreen

This old-fashioned remedy is good for just about everything, but is especially noted as a remedy for rheumatism, diabetes, and bladder troubles. Wintergreen makes a very fine liniment which would be useful for joggers whose legs and muscles need something to ease the pain. A poultice can be made that is good for boils and it can be made into a douche to combat infections in the vagina. If you have a sore throat, consider gargling with wintergreen as it's both refreshing and beneficial.

Wood Sage

Wood sage is useful for wiping and easing sores. And it is one ingredient in a useful poultice for cancer. Add some comfrey and it should be helpful. Use good judgment, however, and don't try to treat cancer by this means without seeing a doctor and going through the traditional cure. I recommend remedies for cancer only when every avenue that modern medicine has been explored and rejected. Wood sage is also good for palsy, and since there isn't a reliable cure for this disease, you might try this remedy to see how it does.

Yarrow

This plant is recommended for measles and chickenpox in children, but be sure you have the child seen by a physician if the yarrow doesn't clear up the condition quickly. It's also very good for diarrhea and even in babies it's a remedy. Just be sure the diarrhea is simple and not a symptom for a more complex ailment or disease.

VI

Herbs and Amulets

Abscesses

You can make carrot or potato poultices to treat abscesses, or use lobella or slippery elm. But the best advice for abscesses, have it professionally looked at by the doctor who may decide to lance them, or in other words, provide modern medicine for the condition. You don't want the abscess to grow so seek medical help early in the condition. To help with the abscess destruction process, make an amulet of a black suede pouch in which you put a string of seed pearls and a piece of coral (again, Indian jewelry uses coral often in its designs). Wear the pouch till the abscess is gone.

Aches

Skullcap and peppermint are recommended for aches that aren't connected to arthritis and some other organic disease. The aches we're talking about here, come with age, and herbs are very helpful in treating aches of this nature. You should also wear an amulet to ward off aches. Find an Indian amulet of turquoise and wear it for good health. The turquoise is especially effective when worn around the neck and it is known for being a healing stone. I always wear turquoise, and I can assure you I'm at the age when aches and pains are prevalent. Try it and see if you don't immediately feel better.

Adenoids

Trouble with adenoids may be avoided by treating the condition with bloodroot or golden seal. Sometimes the adenoids have to come out if the condition is bad, so see a doctor about them. Throughout the ordeal of not only having the condition, but also having it relieved, carry an amulet made especially for promoting health. Take a black silk purse—you should make these pouches yourself—and put in it a diamond earring and a piece of onyx stone (Indian jewelry is frequently made with onyx). Add a sprig of rosemary and thyme to the bag. Now put it about your throat and wear it till the adenoid problem has been successfully resolved.

Anemia

Here's a condition that you can treat either by doctor's prescription or herbalist advice. You may make and drink teas from the dandelion, comfrey, raspberry leaves, and others, and help regain your blood's strength after a period of appropriate treatment. Anemia can also be treated with across-the-counter vitamins that contain iron, but you need medical advice on how much to take—probably one pill a day. Anemia, among other things, makes you very tired, so it's an unpleasant condition in that sense. Be sure you treat the anemia so it won't get worse and cause other complications.

Appendicitis

As anybody who knows anything about diseases will tell you, appendicitis is a life-threatening condition and has to be remedied by a physician. Don't go to an herbal doctor because he can't prescribe herbs that do the job that removing the appendix will do. The life-threatening aspect of the condition is that if your appendix ruptures, it poisons your blood and you well could die. So if you feel any sharp pain on the lower right-hand side of your stomach, see your doctor at once to make certain your appendix isn't going. There are herbs to take afterward for the condition (perhaps while it's healing) and these include vervain and buckthorn bark. And you'll want to carry an amulet with you at all times. Put in a brown suede bag a feather from a bird's nest (doesn't matter what kind), and a piece of lapis lazuli. Wear the brown bag amulet until the healing process is complete.

Appetite

If you find your appetite to be small and you normally have a hearty one, then see a physician and find out if this isn't a symptom of some other disease. If it's not, then treat small appetite with chamomile or strawberry tea. You should also make an amulet to carry with you to increase your appetite. In a brown silk bag (just a few inches square), put a real pearl (could be an earring) and a four-leaf clover. If you don't want to spend the time looking for a four-leaf clover, then cheat and go to a flower shop which sells clover of the four-leaf kind. Carry your amulet with you for a week, and with the treatment of herbal tea to add to its power, you should return to a healthy appetite again.

Asthma

There are many treatments for asthma, and wild cherry, masterwort, and comfrey are just a few of the herbs to use for it. If you have a bad case, be sure to make an amulet to aid the healing process and see a doctor who may provide you with antihistamines or other medications to control it. The amulet I recommend is a silver satin bag into which is put a robin's eggshell (your children may have one stashed away among their treasures) and a gold key, which may be a charm on a bracelet. In fact, you can use the whole bracelet as the amulet ingredient rather than taking the key off the chain. Wear your satin bag around your waist under your clothes to ensure that the asthma won't be severe, but as I said if it is severe, see your doctor.

Backache

Besides Doan's Pills and aspirin there aren't many over-the-counter medications that compete favorably with home remedies. Of course, there are plenty of prescription painkillers. Since this is the case, try pennyroyal or tansy in teas and see if they don't clear up your backache with ease. I hope you take into consideration that backaches may indicate that something else, and possibly more dangerous, is wrong with you and medical advice should be sought. But if you know what's causing your backache—such as lifting something heavy—then go ahead and try the tea prescription. Wear an amulet of topaz (a ring will do) to help ease your ache.

Bed Sores

Bed sores can be treated by using a poultice of plantain or balm of Gilead or golden seal and an amulet of a bouquet of anemone flowers on your night stand. The flowers are magical and good to have around when you have a condition such as bed sores that need attention.

Bile

Bile is what comes up from your stomach when you're nauseated. It's a terrible experience to get the taste of bile in your mouth, so you need to watch your food and drink levels to avoid this unpleasant condition. Celandine cleanses the gallbladder of bile, but I wouldn't use this treatment without the explicit instructions of an herbal doctor. You really don't want to do anything to disturb this delicate organ without your physician's knowledge. To increase bile incidentally, hops are recommended. If you need more bile, wait to be diagnosed by a physician to be sure this is true. During this period, carry about with you a blue topaz in a midnight blue satin bag. Add to the topaz a half moon in silver, and a red rose. The amulet should help you cleanse your system and rev it up depending on what you're doing to yourself.

Biliousness

This is an extremely gassy state and requires strong action. Red sage is excellent for treating the condition or a cup of chamomile tea. Sprigs of hyssop and agrimony should be put in a green silk pouch with an Indian animal charm, and the condition should immediately become eased. You might try your herb doctor for a remedy for your condition if, say, the chamomile doesn't relieve it immediately. But red sage is supposed to be the cure for this condition, so start out by taking a tea of it before asking for professional advice.

Bladder

Juniper berries, beech, and chamomile are exellent herbs to use to cure yourself of bladder troubles. Obviously, if they're intense, you'll see a doctor. But if you have simple problems like slow urination, then try a home remedy first. Take a green wool sack that you make and put in it sprigs of wintergreen, water pepper, and the root of a pond lily, plus a silver Indian wedding ring, and see if your condition isn't helped. If the illness persists, then you should seek medical advice.

Blood Purifier

Every now and then, herbal doctors and vegetarians recommend that your blood be purified and the detritus of living be expunged from your arteries. To do this, you need to treat yourself with dandelion, hyssop, red clover, sassafras, and a dozen other herbs in teas. While you're in the process of doing this, wear an amulet of red flannel shaped as a pouch and put in it blood coral (found in the Caribbean) and a pearl (may be a real pearl earring). The combination of the amulet, which you should wear for several days, and the herbs to cleanse your system will have you feeling chipper and less tired than you have been in a long time.

Boils

Some people do get boils and the cure is a poultice of bur-dock, chickweed, or lobelia, among many others, to reduce the swelling. If it has to be lanced, see a doctor, but the poul-tices may very well take the boil and shrink it. It's certainly worth seeing if home treatment can cure the condition.

Bowels

Be very careful with bowel troubles because, as a friend of mine has discovered, it could mean you have diverticulitis. This requires a major operation to get over and months of uncomfortable healing. So if you're just having trouble with bowel movements, carry a dark blue silk bag with a dandelion flower, witch hazel, and myrrh as well as a child's tooth (one the Tooth Fairy took after leaving a dollar under the sleeping child's pillow). This should help you with your bowel condi-tion, but if it doesn't, don't hesitate to get an expert opinion on what is wrong with you.

Breasts

Try comfrey or parsley if your breasts become sore for no apparent reason beyond your exercising too strenuously. Carry (or wear) an amulet made of jade (a figurine in jade is ideal).

Bronchitis

To help in the curing of this often serious illness, take teas made of cubeb berries, mullein, or sanicle, among many oth-ers, and follow your doctor's orders about taking antibiotics. What is so terrible about bronchitis aside from leading directly to pneumonia is that it repeats and repeats itself seemingly for the rest of your life, and you have to deal with it whenever you get a cold. You can't have a simple cold anymore, you have bronchitis. And the first hint of a sniffle means that I, as a sufferer, go immediately to the doctor for a nose spray and antibiotics. But there's nothing that says you can't ease your complaint with a supplement of soothing tea. It's also wise to wear an amulet if you do have bronchitis in its recurring form. I have one made up of a goose feather, and a turquoise ring in a white silk pouch, and wear it whenever I have bronchitis. It helps speed the recovery process. All these amulets are meant to quicken the recovery of whatever ails you. And they do work.

Bruises

If you are the victim of an unsightly bruise, you might try to heal it with comfrey, hyssop, or Saint-John's-wort—just a few of the remedies. To help the healing process, wear an amulet made with a violet satin bag with two violets and a jade piece in it. The violet and green will help draw the bruise away from under your skin and you can make a poultice of your herbs to draw the color away, too.

Burns

Chickweed, burdock, and comfrey are just a few of the herbs that can be used as a poultice for burns. Make certain that your burn is kept cold with ice so that it won't blister. And while you're doing that, wear an amulet of a diamond ring on a silver chain. Diamond is a magical stone and especially powerful when it comes to healing. Wear your diamond regularly and see how healthy you stay.

Cancer

Here are a few suggested herbs for cancer. Blue violet, cleavers, red clover, and dandelion. As you know from what I've said about cancer and home remedies earlier in this book, I don't really feel that you should throw modern medicine to the wind and count on home remedies to cure you. The cure will just not happen and you may lose precious time in bringing the cancer to the attention of a physician who may be able to help. But you, very definitely, need to have a powerful amulet to wear if you have cancer. Put into a red satin sack a piece of coal, a turquoise and silver ring, and a red rose. Wear the sack for three days and three nights, and on the fourth day, bury the red rose in dirt near your back door. Then get a yellow rose and put it in the sack with the other ingredients. Wear the sack again for three days and three nights, and on the fourth night, bury the coal and the yellow rose by your back doorstep, and wear the ring to bed. Wear the ring as your amulet till the cancer is cured.

Canker Sore

The unpleasant canker sore that we were told as children came from the amount of candy we ate, can be treated by using golden seal, red raspberry, or white water lily, among lots of other herbs and plants. Gargle with the teas that you make and soon the sore will be just an unpleasant memory. When you have a canker sore, you also need to have an amulet to assist the home remedies do their work. Take a silver ring and put it on a silver chain. Each day, add another silver ring to the necklace until the sore is gone. The rings don't have to be plain; they may be Mexican snake rings, for example. But it's good to have a collection of rings around anyway because they're used in some powerful health as well as love amulets.

Chest Mucus

If the cough has gotten into your chest, then mucus may come up. You need to treat your chest for more than just a cough that comes with a light cold. Hyssop, sassafras, and wild cherry all make effective teas when it comes to lungs. And an amulet of a gold wedding band owned by your grandparents and worn on your ring finger helps heal your condition. Recite the following spell over your ring before putting it on: "Come away from my immortal soul, oh sickness, and tie yourself up in this wedding knot of a ring to leave me be." Once the lung problems have eased, take the wedding ring and sprinkle it with rosewater to purify it from the illness. Keep it in a white satin box until the next time you need to use it.

Childbirth

These days we follow the orders of an obstetrician when we are pregnant, but some people still live out in the hinterlands and have a midwife on whom to rely. She may prescribe blue cohosh to bring on the labor pains, squaw vine to make the childbirth easier, and a tea of red raspberry leaves and orange to do the same. To wear an amulet that makes certain all goes well, try a sack of white silk with your wedding ring in it and violet (if it's spring) or a marigold (if it's fall), with blood pricked from your ring finger on a piece of cotton. You should also take a lock of your husband's hair and put that in with the amulet. Your childbirth should be easy and no problems should occur from it.

Chills

People that have low blood pressure often suffer chills, and it can be very unpleasant. I, for one, have low blood pressure and suffer from the cold even when it's sixty degrees outside. So I bundle up. But if the chills stem from a common cold, you may wish to treat them. For the shivers I get from the cold, I sometimes use this amulet too, so I know that it works. Take a white sack and into it put a piece of silver wire. Add a carved animal stone made by the American Indians, and a white chrysanthemum flower. Use it while making teas of cayenne pepper plant, peppermint, and peach, and keep yourself wrapped up in a blanket. The chills should pass quickly, but if they don't and they turn into convulsions, see a doctor for whatever else ails you.

Circulation

Cayenne, witch hazel, and golden seal are all good for circulation problems. If the circulation in your limbs isn't up to par, you'll notice swelling and you should make a poultice of the witch hazel and plaster it on it. You also need an amulet to get your blood flowing normally. So take a piece of bayberry bark and wrap it in light blue satin with several bayberries, add a piece of coral, and wear it until your circulation makes an improvement. The amulet should hurry along the cure the poultice gives and your legs or arms should return to normal quickly. Naturally, if they don't, see a doctor as soon as possible. Problems with circulation can be serious and dangerous, and you need to have yours assessed if it doesn't respond to a home remedy.

Colds

Peppermint, ginseng, rosemary, saffron, vervain, and lots of other herbs are great for colds. Just make up a tea and feel better with its warmth. The common cold has no antidote, so you just must let it run its course while taking teas that soothe and wearing an amulet to speed the process of healing. Into a light blue satin bag, place a silver moon with a star caught between its tips (you may have to have this made by a jeweler) and add a small ruby (maybe in a ring) and a small amethyst. If it's spring, put a pansy blossom in the bag; otherwise, a red rose will do. Wear the amulet for a week, and then bury the pansy or the rose underneath a tree. Continue wearing the jewels and silver moon, and by the end of the second week, you may be certain the cold will be gone or at least isn't lingering as colds sometimes do for a third week to a month.

Colon

If you are having difficulties with your colon, you must definitely see a doctor. But if there's nothing wrong and you still experience the same problems, you may consider trying vervain, aloe, or bayberry to see if they help. Usually the doctor finds out what's wrong with you and you don't have to resort to herbs and home remedies. Even if you see the doctor, though, wear the following amulet to make the diagnosis not serious and the troubles small ones. Take a black silk sack and put a piece of coal in it. Then add a housefly with a needle through it, and a pentagram carved in a piece of wood. With this tiny amulet, you will be safe from serious harm and difficulties with your health.

Constipation

Here's a condition that yields itself well to home remedies or over-the-counter medication. Among the remedies are chickweed, ginger, rhubarb root, and blueflag. Make a tea and soon the constipation will lessen. To help the home remedies to work swiftly, wear an amulet made of navy blue silk and put in it a pearl (maybe a necklace or earring) a tea rose and a blue parakeet feather (if the bird you find is green, then a green feather). The amulet should be worn whenever consti-pation comes your way and keep it on for a period of twelve hours. Get rid of the parakeet feather and rose at the end of the twelve hours by taking them to a crossroads and throwing them to the winds there. Doing this will assure that the con-stipation is not a symptom of something worse. If the augurs are wrong, however, and the constipation continues, then find out from a doctor if you have a more serious condition.

Coughs

My supervisor has gut-wrenching coughs which he swears are due to a sinus condition. If you are like him, I recommend you use a tea of borage, marjoram, or rosemary, among oth-ers, and wear an amulet of black satin with a piece of ebony, bloodroot, and a sugar cube to keep the cough from taking over your life. The cough I'm talking about comes from smok-ing, so stop. Or perhaps it comes with a cold. In any case, when needed use the amulet as you do the teas, and see if you don't find relief soon.

Cramps

Any sort of cramping, be it in your legs or in your abdomen during menstruation, can be alleviated by drinking a tea of cayenne, fennel, wood betony, or half a dozen other herbs or plants. But you also need an amulet of a healing nature if the cramping persists and for the herbs to do their work in a hurry. Make a bag of pink silk and into it put a sapphire (may be in a ring), a piece of coral (I have some that my grandmother had), and a small horseshoe (may be made of any material). The amulet draws the cramp with the horseshoe pulling on it, and the coral and sapphire keep it to release once you've taken the amulet off. So be sure to just wear it for the length of the cramping. It shouldn't be long once you've started treating the cramp with your herbal teas. You may try using thyme if the other teas don't work quickly. And if none of these eases the condition, see a doctor as cramping sometimes indicates you have diverticulitis. So be sure you're not really suffering from a serious disorder when you have your cramps, especially in the stomach and certainly if it isn't the time of the month for you.

Dandruff

If this is the only condition you have, you're indeed a very lucky human. Some people really suffer from dandruff, and use over-the-counter shampoos that work very well on the stuff. But you may wish to try an herbal remedy for the condition. Sage is effective if you want to treat the dandruff; mix it with shampoo so that you can thoroughly rub the sage through your hair. You don't need an amulet for dandruff outside of wearing a flower in your lapel to brighten up your appearance after the embarrassment of having your clothes covered with the stuff.

Deafness

If you feel that you're going deaf and the doctor confirms it, then you'll want to treat your condition as well as do whatever else he suggests. Always tell a doctor what your plan is so he'll learn something about home remedies. You may treat your condition with tea made of marjoram, or dab oil of wintergreen or rosemary oil into your ears with a cotton swab. You need to make an amulet of a silver coin in a silver sack (made of satin) and add a dandelion and a lily of the valley. Change the flowers every three days during the summer and bury them beneath a tree by some water. In winter, use a white carnation and a white rose to carry in your sack. The flowers will remove the influence of deafness and leave you feeling nurtured and cared for.

Delirium

If you have delirium, and are completely mad, then you need to treat yourself with whatever the doctor prescribes for you along with a tea of hops, hyssop, or valerian. These will soothe you and calm your delirium tremens, which you can get from drinking and at a very advanced stage of alcoholism. In fact, if you are going to stop drinking, and you can't do it on your own, you need to be detoxified professionally. But just follow your doctor's orders. He'll know how to handle the problem. Tell him you're taking a home remedy to go along with any medication he prescribes and see if he says it's okay. If you're an alcoholic with tremens, you need an amulet to wear while you're being treated. This will make the treatment easier for you: take a tiny purple candle, a needle through the wick of it, and put it with the eye of a peacock feather in a purple silk bag. Wear the amulet while you're undergoing recovery. It will also keep you from wanting another drink until you can get to AA and start on the road to recovery.

Diabetes

With this disease, you want to have permission from a physician to treat it with home remedies as well as insulin or whatever you must take for it. If he agrees that teas might help but wouldn't hurt, then try some of saw palmetto berries, wintergreen, dandelion root, blueberries, and leaves. You should also wear, for a year at a time throughout the course of this disease, a light blue satin sack with a gold ring set with a diamond, and a red carnation. Keep the carnation for a period of five days and bury it in a woods near your home. If you live in the city, then a park will do fine for burying the flower. You should chant: "Illness lessen with time and be carried away to the earth in this flower." While doing this ceremony, wear the diamond ring and then make another sack that night and put the ring back in it.

Diarrhea

Marshmallow, peppermint, strawberry, and thyme teas will help if you have diarrhea and don't want to use an over-the-counter medication. If the diarrhea lasts more than a day, then it's probably a symptom of something else and you may need medical attention. Call your doctor first and explain to him what's wrong and what you've been taking. An amulet to wear with this condition is a black silk sack with a silver and turquoise ring, a blue flower of any kind that grows wild in your area, plus your amulet of the moon with the star in its arms. Change the flower every five days by burying it under a tree at midnight and replacing it at once.

Dizziness

If you have vertigo, or the sensation of being dizzy and falling, then you'll want to do as I did, when I contracted it, and go to a doctor. There is medication for vertigo and it works very well. Vertigo is a strange condition because there's no telling how long it will last. Once you get it, it can come back periodically or even permanently and last the rest of your life—or completely disappear. If you want to experiment on it with home remedies, try peppermint tea or tea made of rue. They may be able to help you some, but I think I'd stick with the vertigo pill and maybe take the tea as an adjunct if the doctor agrees that it's okay. When I had the vertigo, I made an amulet that I think was at least partly responsible for the condition never coming back to haunt me. I carried a silver thimble that my grandmother gave me in a poison-green satin sack with a silver heart locket that had my picture in it. The little amulet made it possible for me to continue my life without the dreadful vertigo.

Earache

If you begin to have an earache and need a quick remedy for it, try putting pure squeezed lemon juice into your ear. You may also put the liquid from hops tea in, or perhaps hydrogen peroxide, which is a wonderful home remedy for this condition. You might need an amulet if you often have to treat earaches. Take a piece of light green silk and make a sack with it. Put into your sack a piece of yellowdock and a piece of gingerroot, along with your wedding ring (if you don't have one try to acquire a ring that's been in the family) and wear it for as long as the earache persists. After several days, if the treatment and amulet don't work, then visit a doctor to be sure it's not a serious infection causing the pain.

Eczema

This is still a difficult condition to clear up and a home remedy used on it is a positive influence. Try cleavers, dandelion, or plantain leaves in a poultice. As a child, I had a friend who suffered from eczema, and there really wasn't a cure for it in those days. Since one doesn't hear much about it anymore, I imagine that it's treatable, so check with a physician if you get an outbreak of the rash on your arms. Also, wear a white satin sack and put into it an acorn, a keychain, and a small deer sculpture (may be made of plastic, like the ones used as Christmas ornaments). Carry the amulet till the condition heals, and when it's gone, bury the amulet in your backyard under a tree to purify it for one month. Then you may take the amulet back in the house for use next time if the eczema returns.

Emetics

Here are a few substances that will make you throw up when it's important that you do. Bayberry bark and lobelia in large quantities will cause you to vomit. If you are already vomiting and want to stop, then try peach leaves, peppermint, or spearmint. You might need an emetic if you think a child has swallowed something poisonous, and you may need an anti-emetic if you suddenly start to vomit and don't know why. Naturally, in either case, you should see a doctor right away. During the recovery period, wear a black satin sack with a gold heart (locket will do) and a ruby ring. Put a dandelion in the sack with the jewelry and wear it till the condition has cleared up.

Enema

If you need an enema, you might try one of these home remedies until you go to a doctor to have one prescribed for you. Make a liquid of chickweed, alum root, or strawberry leaves, such as you'd make for a tea, and use it as an enema instead. Put a yellow and a white rose on your nightstand to help the enema to work properly. You will sleep comfortably and without incident if you keep the roses by your bedside.

Epilepsy

Epilepsy is one of those convulsive diseases that can be treated by modern medicine. So if you have epilepsy, take the medication the doctor orders for you, and then ask if it's alright to take home remedy teas to go along with the medicine. If it's okay with your doctor, then you're ready to take skullcap, valerian, or vervain, among the other remedies available. You need to have an amulet in addition that you carry at all times as the epilepsy can strike anytime, anywhere. Make a navy blue satin bag, and into it put a blue topaz ring, an African violet flower, and a photograph of yourself. After wearing the amulet for a week, take out the flower and burn in the flame of a midnight blue candle. Scatter the ashes over the nearest stream, and replace the flower with a fresh one. This will help keep the epilepsy at bay until your corrective medications take effect.

Eyes

If your eyes are inflamed, you probably need to be medically treated. But if you can't get to an eye doctor right away and need to treat the condition, then use borage, fennel, or rosemary made into an eyewash. Sassafras makes a good eyewash, as does wintergreen. You'll need a purple sack to make your amulet. Put into it a silver and turquoise ring or other piece of jewelry with a turquoise in it, and an American Indian amulet animal (these are tiny animals carved from stone). Put an Indian paintbrush flower in your sack, and wear the amulet for several days, or at least until the condition is cleared up.

Fainting

If you have a fainting spell, inform your doctor as it could be an important symptom of something if you begin to feel worse and worse. Meanwhile, it's very important to carry an amulet to keep you from having another spell. Take a black silk sack, and into it put the pentagram written in blood (gently pricked from your finger) on a piece of parchment. Then put a ring of pink pau shell in, along with a four-leaf clover. Wear it for a week at a time and then replace the clover. You'll want to keep this up for several weeks to make certain you aren't going to have another fainting spell.

Female Complaints

If you have a discharge, then by all means go to the gynecologist and get rid of it right away. Women who just let vaginal infections worsen without the aid of modern medicine sometimes get candida albicans, which, once in the bloodstream, is almost impossible to get rid of. For a discharge, you need the appropriate ointment from the doctors to heal the condition. You might also try teas of squaw vine, yarrow, or comfrey. There are a variety of cures, but these are three good ones. To guard against candida albicans and other female troubles, carry a pink silk sack with a turquoise in it and a silver comb. Use the comb to do your hair and put the hairs from the comb into your sack. At the end of your treatment for the condition, put the hairs you've collected in a pile and burn them with a pink candle. Throw the ash on the nearest stream and save the amulet sack till the next time you need it.

Fever

You have to be awfully sure what kind of fever you have as it could easily mean you have a serious infection somewhere that needs treatment. But if you know what's causing it, try taking sarsaparilla, parsley, or peppermint teas to break up the fever. Also, carry a white silk sack to bed with you, and into it put a rose (white), a nickel, and a penknife. When the fever is gone, bury the rose in the middle of your backyard, and put the amulet away until you need it again.

Gargle

I've written before of other gargles, and the ones I give this time are specifically to remove bad breath. This can be an ordeal of a condition as it returns so quickly, but a trip to the dentist may reveal a rotting tooth or peridontal disease which is causing the bad breath. A gargle of hyssop, myrrh, or sage should help keep your breath reasonably fresh till the dentist finds out what's ailing you. If you feel you need an amulet to keep your dental condition from being critical, then make one of bronze satin, with a stone of lapis lazuli, and a blue flower (either wild or cultivated). After the gargle has worked its magic and you've been diagnosed by the dentist, then bury the flower (after you've healed) in the ground by your front step. Chant over it: "Keep the toothache and bad breath away from my door. Stop the evil spirits who bring disease and capture them in your dead petals." That should take care of your mouth problems for a while.

Gallstones

Gallstones are very painful if you don't have them removed. These days you can have them broken up with laser or other modern surgery. But if old time surgery is necessary, then ask if you may take healing teas before the operation. If the doctor sees no harm in it, drink chamomile tea, cherry bark, or rhubarb teas, and see if they don't make some of the pain go away. If the pain subsides, the doctor may decide not to do an operation at this time and wait to see if the stone passes. If it doesn't, then you'll have to undergo the medical treatment for your own safety and welfare. Also, wear an amulet of topaz (yellow) in a yellow silk sack, and the healing process will be enhanced.

Gas

If you have excessive amounts of gas, and need a home remedy to adjust and regulate the flow, then have a cup of anise tea, or peppermint, sage, or thyme, and a variety of others that you can get from your health food store. Gas is a most unpleasant condition, and needs to be taken care of as quickly as possible, so take your remedy regularly. A small amulet of jade should be worn to help rid yourself of the excess gas. The amulet can be in the form of a monkey or an Oriental priest. And you should dip the amulet in rosewater and speak over the charm as you do: ''Jade keep away my illness and cleanse my body of all ailments   After the jade is thus purified for its purpose, then wear it around your wrist till the gassy condition is gone.

Genitals

If you have burning or itching genitals, this may be a sign that you have venereal disease, so be awfully certain that you know where the itching comes from. If it was from a sexual encounter that was a bit too bouncy, then go ahead and use a home remedy to alleviate the discomfort. Raspberry leaves made into a tea or even as a poultice will help with the condition. And you can take a tea of pleurisy root that will help, too. Chickweed may be used as a wash, so instead of using it as a tea, turn it into a wash for the genital area. You may be especially sensitive about conditions of the genitals and want to wear an amulet to protect them from disease. Make a sack of light green silk, and into it put a piece of turquoise for strong good health, along with a shamrock. Also add a small silver horseshoe that you may have to have a jeweler make for you. The amulet is strong and good for your general health as well a that of your genitals, and you may wear it whenever you think your body may be threatened with an unpleasant condition.

Gonorrhea

Here's a venereal disease that you really need to treat with antibiotics in a doctor's office. The only excuse for not doing this is that you live in a rural area where you can't easily get to a doctor. If this is the case, then use temporary measures by making burdock tea, cubeb berries, or golden seal. These will help the condition from getting too severe, until receiving medical attention. Also, wear a black suede bag with an image of the person who gave you the disease, and a small pencil, sharpened, and a small piece of parchment with that person's name written on it with yours under it. Put the parchment in the bag, and when you've been successfully treated for the disease, burn the paper and the pencil and vow never again to see the person who gave you gonorrhea.

Hair

There are really no medicines yet for growing back a full head of hair, although there are signs that one may be developed soon. So don't get carried away with ads that tell you your hair will grow back if you use a certain product—theirs. But if you insist on trying to grow it back, try rubbing Indian hemp into your scalp and see if there's a difference. Sage and peach are very good for keeping hair from falling out, if that's your trouble, so you want to make a poultice of them for your hair. Meanwhile you can carry an amulet that keeps your hair from being traumatized to the point where it starts to fall out. Take a piece of royal blue satin and make a little drawstring sack from it. Into it put a baby's tooth, a locket with a picture of you as a child, and a snippet of baby's hair (yours if you still have some). It doesn't matter what child this comes from, but it's best, of course, if the hair belonged to you. Wear the amulet during the period you're trying to grow hair, or at least keep it from falling out any more. It should help you stop the process of balding, and the charm works just as well for women as it does for men.

Hayfever

Here's a condition that can be cured by going to your doctor and getting antihistamine shots and tablets. You really had better consider doing that before getting involved with home remedies. With your doctor's permission use these in conjunction with his prescribed medication. Coltsfoot is an effective remedy for hayfever. Also make a sack of white cotton and into it put one piece of jade and one of turquoise. Add a chrysanthemum, if you're not allergic to it, and carry the amulet during the hayfever season.

Headache

Here's a condition that has a lot of remedies. My favorites are teas made of peppermint, rosemary, rue, and thyme. If you periodically have headaches and know they're not a symptom of something else but probably just congested sinuses, then go ahead and use one of these home remedies on yourself. Also, make an amulet to help rid yourself of the condition. Into a dark blue silk sack put a piece of brain (what you can find at the meat counter at the supermarket is fine), a vial of rosewater, and a small silver hammer that you can have made by a jeweler. It's worth it to put this amulet together if you're bothered by nagging headaches. But if you suddenly start getting headaches out of nowhere, you need to see a doctor about them as they may indicate something else is wrong with you.

Heart

Borage is used to make the heartbeat strong, while cayenne is used as a stimulant if it's weak. I can hardly think of anyone with a serious heart condition who would just count on home remedies to make him well, so you must follow your doctor's orders as well. Given the nature of the remedies, I would tell him that you're drinking teas with these substances so he'll know what to tell you about them. He may not want you to stimulate your heart and therefore cayenne wouldn't be an appropriate herb to use. Peppermint is also used for heart conditions as are sorrel, valerian, and motherwort. If you choose any of these, let your doctor know. And wear the amulet I suggest for heartburn and it will protect you from further difficulties that might arise while you're in the healing process.

Heartburn

Heartburn differs from gas in that the pain comes up around the area of your heart and in your throat. Gas pains generally stay in the abdomen and lower intestines. But one of the worst kinds of pain that does nothing so much as make you think you're having a heart attack is heartburn, so it must be gotten rid of right away. You can take Mylanta or any of the other antacids over-the-counter to rid yourself of the discomfort, or you can have a home remedy do the trick. Angelica or burnet are excellent remedies if you make a tea of them, and you must wear an amulet that assists the condition to go away. Find yourself a miniature Bible (about an inch square, maybe two inches) and put it into a white satin sack with a piece of violet incense. Add a gold wedding band and wear the amulet to protect you against heartburn and all the heart diseases. If you have had a heart attack, this amulet will work for that condition as well.

Hemorrhoids

Some of these hemorrhoids aren't bad enough to require surgery and can be treated with over-the-counter medicines. But you may wish to try a home remedy that might do as well as Preparation H, and be more comforting. Shepherd's purse, yarrow, and aloe can be used to treat the condition, and you may wish to make an ointment. Aloe should be especially good in an ointment as it's very healing and the remedy I recommend most here for the condition. If you have an aloe plant, bruise the leaf and the liquid can be used right on the site of the hemorrhoids without surgery. Try an amulet made of clippings from a horse's hoof and a strand from its mane. Wind the strand of hair around a silver ring (plain) and put the items in a black silk bag which you should wear during the hemorrhoid flare-up. Once they're quiet again, then you may stop wearing the amulet.

Hiccoughs

Here is a nasty condition that occurs once in a while— hiccoughs that just won't stop. I use the bartender's method of bitters and lemon and it always works. But you may use dill to control it, and even orange juice is a fine remedy. But to keep you from getting the hiccoughs in the first place, wear a charm of woodbine and lily of the valley that you make in the spring from your garden. Add to it a robin's egg that you might find on the grass. With this amulet in a white silk sack, you'll never have trouble with hiccoughs again. It's been known to stop the condition so it's a powerful amulet to keep. Make a fresh amulet each spring, and when you suffer this spasmodic attack, pull it out and wear it and you'll feel much better.

High Blood Pressure

Here's a condition affecting lots of people, who are taking pills to control it. Ask your doctor if it's alright to combine modern medication with teas that might help your high blood pressure, and then try hyssop, valerian, and wild cherry bark. These are three strong remedies, so be sure you ask for a medical opinion before taking them. You also need an amulet to wear to keep your pressure stabilized. Try a purple satin sack with a ruby in it (maybe a ring), a red carnation and a piece of blood coral (you can find on the beach in the Caribbean or from a rockhound's store). Carry the amulet so long as you have the high blood pressure and change the red carnation once a week. Bury the old bloom near a fork in the road. And chant: "Flower so pure, keep my illness with your death safe in the earth." Do the burying at midnight and you should find your pressure lowering in a short time.

Hoarseness

I have a friend who smokes a great deal and used to drink a lot as well, and has a hoarseness. So I have recommended that she try wild cherry tea, mullein, or coltsfoot. As a result, her hoarse voice has gone away and she sounds worlds better. I also made her an amulet to carry that protects against voice problems. Take an orange sack made of silk, and into it put a tiny gold harmonica (you may be able to find a charm that's just right), an aquamarine stone (may be in a ring), and a spring violet. The violet doesn't have to be blooming to be used, but you should have the plant in your house at all times as it brings good luck. Wear the amulet till the hoarseness is gone, then put it away for future use.

Hydrocephalus

This is a condition of water on the brain that most surgeons find difficult or impossible to treat. You can get "wet brain" from drinking alcohol too much. Since there isn't much that can be done once developed, you might rely on a home remedy if someone you know has the condition. Red sage, marjoram, and rosemary teas are recommended individually, and you can combine these as well to make an even stronger libation. I doubt if the home remedy will have the effect of curing hydrocephalus, but it might ease the suffering

somewhat. I know that with "wet brain" caused by alcoholism, there is little hope once you've gotten it.

Hysteria

I've given remedies for hysteria and they're good ones but
you need an amulet for the condition as well as medication.
Saffron made into a tea is effective, and pennyroyal and rue
are also fine remedies. An hysteric needs to be calmed as
quickly and as much as possible before they need a sedative to
do the trick. If the hysteria comes back from time to time, then
an amulet to fight it off needs to be worn. Take a yellow satin
sack and put in a black onyx stone, a tulip bulb for a red tulip,
and a photograph of yourself when you're calm and smiling.
If you're not the one with the hysteria, put a photo in of the
person that does have it. The amulet will protect against hysteria and ease it somewhat if it does come back.

Indigestion

I've mentioned this condition before so I'll say again that
bay leaves, cayenne, and ginseng all make teas that help
indigestion. These remedies are in place of over-the-counter
products like Alka Seltzer, for those people who don't like the
available store-bought kind. If you often have indigestion, you
want an amulet to wear when it attacks. Take a black suede
sack and into it put an old pocket watch (maybe from your
grandmother or grandfather), three acorns, and a white
chrysanthemum. Wear the amulet every day, or for so long as
the indigestion lasts, and bury the chrysanthemum in your
backyard replacing it every time you use the amulet. Let it lie
without a mum during the periods you're not using it. When
you bury the old one, chant: "Take my illness back to the
earth," as you're digging the hole. And continue the chant as
you cover up the mum. This will help assure that the indigestion doesn't come back. Naturally if you find indigestion with
you a great deal, a doctor might find it to be a symptom for
something else.

Inflammations

Usually if you have an inflammation of some kind, the doctor gives you an antibiotic. But you may also use teas made of fenugreek, sarsaparilla, and hyssop. Check to be sure that the home remedies aren't going to interfere with the workings of the antibiotic. You'll need an amulet to help the inflammation go away. Into a light violet satin sack put a red rose, an American Indian animal amulet, and a piece of pau (the Indians use this stone in their jewelry). Wear the amulet till the inflammation is gone. Bury the rose every three days by a crossroads and rotate between yellow rose and red rose each time you use the amulet for this condition.

Influenza

There aren't many cures recommended for the flu, but teas made with Indian hemp, peppermint, and white pine are recommended for the condition. You might do just as well with home remedies as you would with an expensive prescription from a doctor. But you definitely need an amulet while you have the flu. Take a silver satin sack, and into it put a nickel, a needle with silver thread poking into a strawberry, and a silver wedding ring from the American Indians. When the strawberry spoils after a few days, bury it in the front yard near your steps, and chant: "Fly away flu to the earth."

Insanity

As we all know, insanity is just now being treated with modern miracle drugs, and you should follow your psychiatrist's advice when they are prescribed. You can't drink with these drugs, and they need to be made just right for your condition. But it may be possible, with your doctor's permission, to take teas made from peppermint, rosemary, or rue that will soothe you and not take away from the medication. Be sure before taking a tea with a psychotropic drug, however. The amulet you'll need in the case of mental illness is yellow silk for a sack, a gold ring set with a diamond (maybe an engagement ring) and a yellow mum. You may also add a sprinkle of the herbs I've mentioned to round out the effect they have as a tea and as part of an amulet. Bury the mum every few days and add a fresh one. While burying it, chant: "Heal me, oh great God of the Universe." The amulet should bring a least some peace of mind back to you.

Insect Bites

You'll need to make a poultice to treat insect bites, use plantain, pennyroyal, or gentain leaves. There are so many new and dangerous bugs in the United States, that it's wise to know which of them are poisonous and need doctor's care. Ticks are quite dangerous and can leave you comatose if you aren't diagnosed and treated properly. So you are encouraged to dress with socks and jeans tucked inside boots and headgear as well as jackets just to go out in the yard at certain times of the summer. These ticks are suspect now when you exhibit certain symptoms to the doctor, but you are able to treat less dangerous bites with home remedies. If you're going into your yard to cut the grass or cut down bushes and tall weeds, wear heavy gear and take an amulet with you. It should be a green silk sack containing a dead fly with a needle through it, a mosquito, also with a needle through it (possibly on same needle as the fly), and a green colored stone that you've found on your own along a beach. Wear the amulet when you do your yard work and it should be effective to keep dangerous bugs away from you.

Intestines

To treat intestinal conditions, there are all sorts of modern medical methods. But you need to take teas with your condition and with an herb doctor's blessing. Strawberry, mint, and fenugreek make fine treatments. If it doesn't get better then you'll have to submit to modern medical treatments. An amulet that you can wear when undergoing intestinal troubles is an orange silk sack with a pinch of golden seal in it, a small silver bell, and a lilac (pick these in the spring and dry them for use in your amulet all year round). Bury the lilac when the condition disappears.

Itch

Several over-the-counter drugs work with itches effectively but if you don't want to use them, you should try the home remedy. Make a poultice of origanum, yellow dock, or borage, and the itch will soon be under control. These itches are the kinds that come from a bite or a patch of dry skin that you should also be treating with body lotion. Sometimes the lotion isn't strong enough to do away with the itch and that's where your home remedy comes in. Older people suffer from a lot of itches, and these remedies are perfect for them. An amulet to keep away nagging itches (especially if you're older) is made with a yellow satin sack. Into it put a pinch of fresh marjoram, a turquoise earring, and a silver demitasse spoon. Wear the amulet during periods of itching and then bury the marjoram by scattering it on a body of water or a stream near your home. If you don't live near one, scatter it under the water of a sprinkler in your yard. This will take with it the essence of the itch till it next returns and you again need a pinch of marjoram.

Jaundice

If you have jaundice, you are no doubt under a physician's care. See if he'll allow you to treat your condition with home remedies, too. If he doesn't know, check your herbal doctor. Take teas made from dandelion, peach leaves, borage, or chamomile. These may help the condition. Also, wear an amulet made of a red silk sack, a yellow topaz, and a dandelion flower. Put a needle through a bumblebee and add that to the sack (be careful not to get stung). Wear the sack till the jaundice is gone, changing the dandelion once a week and burying it at a fork in the road. Add a new one at that time. You might dry some dandelions for use in amulets during the winter months when they're out of season.

Kidneys

If your kidneys are not in particularly good shape, then it may be time to cleanse them with cayenne, buckbean, parsley, and juniper berries. Make teas of these and drink one in the morning and one in the afternoon. You also need an amulet to go with your tea medications. Take brown silk and sew it into a sack. Then add to it a small vial of your urine, a pocket watch (it doesn't matter if it runs), and a photograph of yourself on a formal occasion. Wear the amulet for as long as you have a kidney condition and empty the urine after the kidneys heal. Don't replace the vial with urine till the next time (if there is one) that you need to wear the amulet.

Laxative

If you need a laxative (here are some more choices since the last mention I made of laxatives), then try peach leaves, wild Oregon grape, or aloe. Any of these will help cleanse the body of its poisons, and will give you a fresh start. You may prefer to take over-the-counter laxatives, but with home-grown ones, any of the above-mentioned substances are good for the purpose. You should have an amulet if you often need laxatives. Take a white silk bag and into it put earrings set with topaz, a fly caught in amber, and a yellow chrysanthemum. Some people swear by a gardenia instead of a mum, but I prefer the latter as they're not so expensive to replace. After you have a bowel movement, just take the chrysanthemum out to a crossroads and bury it in the middle. Naturally the road will have to be dirt, so use some planning about when you go. You don't want to try to bury the flower under macadam.

Liver

If you need to strengthen your liver, which is an organ that can heal, try teas of fennel, parsley, plantain, or aloe. Start taking these teas when warned by your doctor that you'll get cirrhosis if you don't stop drinking. The time to get the liver strengthened is when it's enlarged but capable of returning to normal size. You don't, of course, want to start a regimen of teas without telling your physician, and you should check your herb doctor, too, to see if he recommends these or perhaps some other plants. You'll need an amulet to wear while going through the ordeal of strengthening your liver. Take a sack of yellow satin and into it put a piece of jade in the shape of a monkey, a small bell to keep evil spirits away, and several sprigs of lily of the valley. (Grow these in the spring and then press some for later use.) Wear the amulet for a week at a time and bury the lilies in a flower bed near the front of your house.

Lost Voice

If you lose your voice from laryngitis or some other condition, then try to bring it back with a tea of rosemary, or red pepper, or wild cherry. Treat your voice morning and evening with the tea, and you may even put a poultice around your neck to soothe it. Use the tea cooled off to make the poultice. If this treatment lasts for more than a day, make an amulet of horse hair braided into a bracelet and add a charm to it. The charm should be an American Indian carved animal, and the bracelet should be worn as long as your laryngitis condition lasts.

Lungs

If your lungs are full of phlegm from a cold, then you might try to rid them of the stuff by taking a tea. Comfrey, thyme, and yarrow are all good bets for helping clear your lungs, but you must stop smoking, if you do, because the teas won't work nearly as well. I don't mean to just lightly say "stop smoking" because it is a terrible addiction and hard to stop. All of your concentration must come into full play to stop smoking. Your lungs should be cleared so you won't get worse diseases like emphysema or cancer. You will definitely need an amulet to get you through the phlegm condition for your lungs. Into a pink silk sack put a pearl ring and a pink rose with a pentagram drawn on a piece of parchment. Attach the pentagram to the rose with a needle and add it to your sack. Once your lungs are clear and your cold or bronchitis is gone, then bury the rose and the pentagram and the needle under the pine tree near a crossroads. The next time you need your amulet, make another rose and pentagram combination and you'll feel much better as soon as you start wearing it.

Lumbago

This condition gives you a sore back, and you may want to take a poultice and apply it to the sore spots. Shepherd's purse is recommended, and a poultice is made from the herb boiled in water and a piece of linen to keep it on your back. You can also use vervain and black cohosh to treat the condition. Also, wear an amulet made with a black satin sack containing a shiny new penny, a spider with a needle through it, and an Indian paintbrush, a flower, if you can't buy it in a shop, that must be harvested in the spring and summer for purposes of making amulets. So you'll just have to wait for the right season to collect some of the flowers I call for.

Measles

You'll want to be very careful with your children when it comes to using home remedies on them. Take a child with measles to a doctor first, and if he says you can use herb teas as well to good effect, then go ahead. What works on measles are saffron, red sage, and raspberry leaves. There are more herbs, to be sure, that are effective for measles, but these are the herbs I'd choose. You'll want to make an amulet for your child to wear during the period of measles. If a girl, use pink silk for a sack; if a boy, a blue silk sack should do nicely. Now put a clip of your hair in the sack, and a clip of your husband's. Tie the hairs in either blue or pink ribbon depending on the sex of the child. Now add a ruby ring to the sack and a daisy. When the daisy is three days old, take it out and bury it beneath an oak tree in your yard, then replace it with another if the measles persist. If they're almost healed, then just let the flower go.

Menstruation

I've mentioned herbs before to use with menstruation, but you'll want an amulet to help you while you're adjusting your period. Take a red satin sack, and put into it an empty locket, a small red candle, and a picture of the Virgin Mary. Wear the amulet while you have your period and then put it away in red tissue paper for safekeeping till the next time you'll need it. If you want to drink an herbal tea of red raspberry, that's recommended, too.

Nausea

I've talked about nausea and what to take for it, but I'd like to expand on the subject a bit. Lavender, mint, and peach leaves are good for nausea, but you must, of course, find out if it's a persistent condition and what could be causing it. See a physician. If it's just the result of overeating, then go ahead and treat it with teas. I used to have nausea the next morning if I drank heavily, and the teas can help with that kind of condition, too. If you're prone to nausea, you may want to make an amulet to use when it comes over you. Into a black suede sack put a ring of aquamarine, a picture of yourself as a baby, and an African violet flower. Rather than use spring violets, I recommend the African variety as you can grow them year round in the house. Put a violet into the sack and carry it through the day on which you have nausea. The amulet is meant to protect you from further recurrences of the condition, and you should bury the violet after burning it in a purple candle, putting its ashes beneath a maple tree. If you live out West, you may put it beneath an aspen in Colorado, or beneath an orange tree, if you're in California.

Neuralgia

This condition develops from a pain shooting along a nerve
and all of its branches. And the nerve needs attention to keep
the neuralgia from worsening. Celery tea is one antidote to
the pain; peppermint or wild yam are other teas you may
take. The object is to get the nerve to stop radiating pain
throughout its immediate area. If the teas don't work well,
then see a physician. But I should think that tea treatment and
perhaps a call to the holistic herb doctor to get his ideas on
which to use might do the trick. If you do have neuralgia from
time to time, then you may need an amulet on hand for these
occasions. Make a sack of dark blue velvet (look for silk or
satin velvet) and put into it a real pearl necklace, a pinch of
organum (the herb), and a golden comb. After the neuralgia
has subsided, bury the organum in an African violet pot that
you must keep to supply you through the winter with violets.
Keep the sack without the pearls and golden comb wrapped
in white tissue paper in your dresser drawer, till the next time
you have an attack.

Nervousness

I've discussed nervousness previously, but I want to make
certain you have plenty of ideas of how to treat it and the
recipe for an amulet as well. Nervousness is very unsettling if
you're trying to work at your job or if you're out on an important social or business occasion. You need to calm yourself
(alcohol is not the appropriate antidote, and neither are pills).
Chamomile tea, however, is effective for nervousness and so
are dill or thyme or wild cherry. But you need an amulet to
wear if you do have this serious condition. Make a white velvet sack, and into it put a turquoise ring or earrings (doesn't
matter which), a sprig of mint, and a lace handkerchief. Wear
the sack day and night till your nervousness finally subsides.
At that point, take the dead mint leaf and plant it with the live
ones in your garden. Chant over it as you plant it: "Nervous
to earth through this leaf go." You should keep the next attack
at bay and not so strong with your amulet. Start wearing it
again the moment you feel the nervousness return.

Nightmare

For those of you who have nightmares (you can learn all about them in *The Modern Witch's Dreambook*), then you'll want to get out of bed and fix a tea that will take them away and keep them from coming back. I recommend peppermint tea, or if you prefer, tea made of thyme. Either one will keep you free from nightmares when you return to sleep. If you often have them, then you may need an amulet to wear to bed with you. You may put it under your pillow if you like and it will have the same effect as if you wore it. Put into a sack of pink silk a sprig of lily of the valley, a sprig of catnip, and a housefly with a pin through it. The night after the nightmare, take out the lily of the valley and the catnip and put them in a matchbox which you then bury by your back stairs of your house or apartment. If you dig them up the next day and they're still fairly fresh, a vampire has been bothering your sleep and you need to put crosses around your room till the nightmares subside. Also use garlic in the corners of your bedroom if you've ascertained that a vampire is causing you this distress. It may be someone you know who is pulling deviltry on you. So take a close look at your friends: one may be a vampire.

Nightsweats

This can be caused by a vampire as well as nightmares. This condition also can be the result of drinking alcohol over a period of time. If you stop, the nightsweats will disappear on their own. If something else is causing them, see a doctor. But if they're the simple sweats, then take a tea of strawberry leaves. Make an amulet of a black satin sack with a piece of garlic, a cross, and a picture of the person you think is the vampire causing you these troubles. Wear it for at least two weeks until the nightsweats subside.

Nosebleed

If you happen to get one because you picked at your nose and started the bleeding, then you may stop it with witch hazel or wild alum root. Find out from your herb doctor which he recommends and go ahead and use it. Bayberry bark is also effective, so check with him on that, too. If your nosebleeds emanate from another source, you'll have to check a doctor to see if they're a symptom of something worse. If you wish, with a simple nosebleed, you can take a cold wash-cloth and put it on the back of your neck with your head tilted back. This is the remedy I use and it works when I have a simple nosebleed.

Obesity

You'll need to see a nutritionist to put you on a proper diet if you've let yourself grow into obesity. And let the doctor know that you also want to take a course of teas to help you lose weight. Tell him you want to make teas of fennel, bur-dock, or sassafras, and see what he says. If he's negative, check with your herb doctor to see what he says about treat-ing the overweight with teas. Also, make yourself an amulet to wear as you're in the process of weight loss. Make a yellow velvet sack, and into it put a bar of chocolate, a thimble, and a picture of you when you were thin. The chocolate should act as an antidote to your cravings when you say the proper words over your amulet: "Sugar away from me, pounds of fat to earth with you." Once you have returned to a weight you plan to keep for awhile, then bury the candy bar in the earth by a river or well-flowing stream. Repeat the spell and you should stay as thin as you want.

Pain

If you have the kind of extended pain that often arthritis causes, then you will want to know about home remedies for dealing with it. Teas to soothe you include mint, chamomile, and dill. One or two teas a day will keep the pain level controllable. You'll want to have an amulet against pain as well. Get a golden chain and hang from it a pendant made of turquoise (this is the strongest antidote for pain among the magical stones) and a gold wedding band that has been handed down in your family. If you can't find one from your family, then you'll have to purchase one new in a jewelry store. Say over the charm as you're putting it on: "Pain to stone, save me." And don't neglect to have a crucifix somewhere in your bedroom as a reminder to pray to God to help relieve your terrible pain.

Palsy

It's very difficult to find a medication that's really good for palsy, so you may as well use a home remedy to help. Skullcap, wood betony, and elder all are home medications for the condition, but you'll need an amulet to help them do their work. Make a pentagram on parchment (from a stationery store) by pricking your finger and using the blood to draw it. Put your name and GOD inside the pentagram using blood for the letters. Bury the parchment in your garden by the light of the moon at midnight, and chant over it: "Blood to earth, take my palsy from me," and you should start feeling better almost immediately. If you have need of making other parchments later on, do make them. The power of a parchment charm lasts about two weeks.

Pancreas

If you are having difficulties with your pancreas, I suspect you've been to a doctor who has diagnosed the problem. Ask if it's okay to use a home remedy, and then try a tea of dandelion or blueberry leaves. Make an amulet of two strands of horsehair and an ivory elephant charm which you put on the strands before braiding them. The charm should work against further harm to your pancreas, and keep you a lot less sick than you might have been.

Piles

Piles are hemorrhoids (just another name for them) and you definitely need an amulet to wear against their pain. Some hemorrhoids are so painful that they must be operated on. But if you have just a small but irritating case of them, then you need an amulet as well as such remedies as Solomon's seal, spearmint, or witch hazel. So here is an amulet to wear when you're having an attack of piles. Take an earth brown satin sack, and put into it a pair of sewing scissors (the kind that you use to clip thread). If you can get them in silver, all the better. Sometimes antique stores will carry the little scissors I'm talking about. My grandmother and mother had them and passed them along to me so I have mine ready for amulets. Then you'll want to add to the sack, a chicken feather (down from a baby chick is best), and a baby tooth. Chant over the contents: "Piles to dust, in the ground they must go." Then wear your sack for three days and three nights, on the fourth morning, put them in the earth by an oak tree. At the end of the day (around 6:00 P.M.), dig up the sack and take it in the house and disassemble the charm. Your piles should be under control now, and the amulet should be carefully put away to use the next time.

Pimples

What a dread condition pimples are to young men and women! And while the over-the-counter medications for them are constantly improving, it's still good to try a home remedy that is effective. You'll want to make teas of the herbs mentioned, then daub the pimples with the liquid. Try some spikenard, some plantain, or valerian. I've just started using valerian on my husband's back. No longer a teenager, he still gets terrible pimples on his back and sometimes his face, and I have to treat him constantly to keep the pimples from overwhelming him. So if you want to try an herbal remedy to control this condition, then do so.

Pleurisy

The pleures are found in the lung area, and when they become inflamed, then pleurisy develops. You will have to treat this condition medically, but you may also try herb remedies after checking to see that the antibiotics aren't either weakened or strengthened by the herbs. You should try pleurisy root, cayenne, or yarrow, to name a few remedies. And you need an amulet to help clear up the pleurisy. Into a silver pouch made of satin put a white candle with a needle stuck through the wick, a seashell (doesn't matter what kind) and a silver buckle (should be real silver). Wear the amulet till the pleurisy is healed. (Incidentally, you can also use this amulet to treat pimples.) When the conditions are cleared up, remove the pin from the wick of the candle until you again need the amulet.

Pneumonia

Never rely only on teas for pneumonia, which can be extremely serious. But make a sack of black velvet and into it put a silver ring, a silver comb with your hairs in it, and a silver thimble. Over the amulet you chant: "Illness to silver and tarnish keep it." When the pneumonia is gone, polish the silver objects and keep them for other amulets later on.

Quinsy

Quinsy is a severe inflammation of the throat that includes fever and is much like tonsillitis. What you need to soothe your throat are a gargle and teas, using hyssop, sage, raspberry leaves, and cudweed. First use them (individually, not all at the same time) as a gargle, then take as a tea. You shouldn't have more than two teas in a day without an herb doctor's advice. You'll need an amulet while the quinsy heals. Wear an American Indian thunderbird and say over it as you put it around your neck: "Protect me, oh thunderbird, from illness and death." The jewelry should be worn day and night till the quinsy starts healing. But you should also see a physician to get the appropriate antibiotics if needed. And you'll want him to diagnose your condition anyway, so don't neglect going to the doctor and settle just for a home remedy instead.

Relaxants

These are home remedies that make you relax if you're highly nervous about something. Boneset and pleurisy root are appropriate antidotes to a nervous condition. You probably get a case of nerves sometime, so you'll need an amulet to wear when you do get wrought up. Take a yellow silk bag that you make into a sack, and into it put an emerald ring, a four-leaf clover, and a jade arrowhead. (You may have to have a jeweler fashion a jade arrowhead but it doesn't have to be a big stone.) Wear the amulet for a day and a night, then bury the clover in some grass under a spreading shade tree. Chant as you bury the clover: "Plant to dust, my illness with you." You should start feeling better a once. But if one clover over a twenty-four hour period doesn't work well, then make the charm again and keep it up for another twenty-four hours. You should feel normal after this bout.

Rheumatism

I've given you remedies for this condition before, but now I want to give you an amulet you can wear to keep the pain from becoming overwhelming. Besides brewing peppermint tea to soothe you, or wild yam, or sarsaparilla, make an amulet of white silk as a sack, and put into it a thistle flower, an amethyst pin (preferably handed down through the family), and a violet, and say over the charm as you put it on: "Pain to purple, away from me." The combination of teas and the amulet will keep you feeling better before much time passes. If all your doctor is prescribing for you for is Tylenol, then this home remedy is at least as strong as the medication. And with the addition of an amulet, it should be much stronger. If you don't feel you're getting any relief from the amulet, however, try the Tylenol. Whatever works best is what you should always go with and use.

Scalds

If you scald yourself under the hot water tap or from the stove, you need to put your burn in cold water immediately, and then treat it with poultices of a choice of onions, bittersweet, or elder. And if you are constantly burning yourself, then you need an amulet to keep you free of kitchen accidents. Take a white muslin sack, and into it put a small kitchen knife, a pinch of flour, and a pau shell ring purchased from an Indian jewelry dealers. (Pau is used a lot in that genre of jewelry.) The amulet should keep you alert as you go about your kitchen tasks. Put it around your waist over your apron, and you should be safe from scalds and cuts in the kitchen.

Sexual Desire

If you have too great a sexual desire, you may wind up as a friend of mine did by going to Sexual Compulsives Anonymous. He described his condition as constantly thinking about sex. He just didn't have time to think of anything else, nor did he have time to do much else except indulge in sex. A family man, he found the strain intolerable. There are some herbs that reduce the desire for sex and I asked him to try them: hops, sage and skullcap. I also recommended an amulet to wear to keep the sexual urges in check. Into a pink satin sack, I told him to put a pinch of salt, a turquoise ring, and a tiger lily. You may have to go to a florist to get the lily if it isn't spring or summer. He was to say over the amulet: "Keep me clean and pure as the thought of God." Once the impure thoughts have started to go away, then bury the lily under an oak tree at night and say, "Take my unclean life with you to the earth." With the help of support groups, the condition starts getting under control and a normal life can be pursued.

Sinus

If you are having difficulties with your sinuses (as I usually do), then follow my lead and brew a cup of plantain and bring out your amulet for a sinus infection. If you have these infections at least once or twice a year, then you need to make and store an amulet for just such occasions. Take a robin's feather and put it into a green velvet sack with an agate and the flower from a Queen Anne's lace weed. Wear the amulet as long as you have the infected sinus, then store it, minus the flower for the next time. Burn the flower, and scatter the ashes out your front door while chanting: "Illness be death in the sand." You should feel better for your treatment. If you don't, however, and the infection gets worse, see a doctor about antibiotics, as I sometimes have to do, and just realize that modern medicine cures many illnesses that home remedies just can't.

Skin Problems

If you have trouble with infections of the skin (check with your physician to identify what you have), and you want to enhance the job of the antibiotics prescribed, then take teas made of dandelion, saffron, sassafras, or wintergreen. These teas should aid the healing process. Tell your doctor that you're planning to take his medication in combination with your teas, just to be sure there's no conflict between the two. And you'll want to have an amulet to make the healing process go along at a steady but rapid pace. Make a turquoise silk sack, and into it put a pink rose and a piece of turquoise. Add an Indian ring that's shaped like a snake. Wear the amulet for twenty-four hours, then take the flower outside and bury it under a stone near your backdoor step (if you live in an apartment building, you can still bury the rose under a stone near one of its back entrances). As you bury the rose, chant: "Pure skin again, rose take the sickness." Then put a new rose in your sack. Every twenty-four hours take out the flower and put in a fresh one, burying the old one, each time, in the backyard.

Sleep

If you have trouble falling asleep, try vervain, peppermint, or hops to do the trick. A nice peppermint tea should soothe you and put you in dreamland almost at once. And as an amulet to help you sleep, take a gray silk sack and put into it a silver pencil (must be real silver), a silver egg, and a chrysanthemum blossom. With your peppermint tea, and the amulet to help it do its job, you should experience no problem sleeping at will. Later, burn the chrysanthemum blossom and scatter its ashes on the wind, chanting: "Sleep to the earth may I sleep without pain." Then when you need to use the amulet again, get another flower to put in your sack.

Sores

If you have an unusual sore spot such as I sometimes have in the winter months, it's good to have a home remedy available to heal it as it's not big enough to take to the doctor. Still, you don't want to have it infected. Put iodine on it, and then some peach leaves as a poultice. You can take aloe leaves or mullein and do the same. And to keep your body free of these sores that show up during the cold seasons, take a brown silk sack and into it put a walnut, a piece of mistletoe, and a silver locket with your picture in it. During the cold months, wear this about your waist on a thong and make it seem like a piece of jewelry. Your body soon should be completely free of lesions and you should feel much better too.

Sore Gums

This is one for the dentist, no doubt about it, but if you wear false teeth and have sore gums, then a home remedy can help you. Put myrrh or golden seal on your gums and see if they soon don't feel better. Get out your amulet to wear around your neck while experiencing the sore gums: make the amulet of white silk and into it put a baby tooth, a plain silver ring, and a marigold. Keep the marigold for as long as the sore gums last, and when they've healed, take the flower and put it on your nightstand till it's dry and withered. Then burn it with some fall leaves and scatter the ashes. Chant: "Mouth heal in the ashes of the fire where the illness has gone." Sore gums shouldn't be a problem for quite some time after this ceremony. Keep the ingredients nearby, especially if your false teeth are new.

Sore Throat

Here's a condition that is usually a symptom of something worse in the way of an oncoming cold. But sometimes your throat is just a little sore without being a symptom of an illness. When that happens, sore throat drops such as Hall's help, or have a home remedy available. Cayenne or ginger or horehound are three cures for a common sore throat, and if you develop if often enough, you could also use an amulet to speed the cure. Into a red silk sack put an onyx ring (one handed down through the family is best but you may also buy one through Indian jewelry dealers), an African violet blossom, and a hard-boiled egg. When the sore throat is gone, bury the egg and the violet flower in the front yard under a tree. As you do it, chant: "Sickness to egg and violet flower, bury the sore throat with you." You should not have a recurring sore throat for awhile.

Sprain

If you have a sprain, there isn't much the doctor can do but wrap it and tell you to give it a rest. What you need to do is to put a poultice made of comfrey or wormwood on the sprain. Then make an amulet of an orange silk sack. Into it put a lucky penny you've found, a picture of yourself (a current one), and an orchid (a small yellow one is best), and wear it for as long as the pain from the sprain lasts. When it's better, take the orchid and cast it into a stream while chanting: "Away on the water take my pain with you forever." This should insure that the pain won't come back any time soon.

Stimulants

If you've had a very hard day but have a full evening ahead of you, too, and you don't think you can make it, then you might want to take a mild stimulant. Try a tea of cayenne or peppermint or raspberry, and you should feel better at once. It may be that you have a busy schedule every evening after coming home from work and that you need an amulet to help keep you mentally and physically alert. Put a family diamond ring into a black satin sack, and add lily of the valley (a dried one will do if the flower's out of season). Now add a touch of pennyroyal, and a bit of ginger, and wear the amulet as soon as you get home until it's time to start your round of evening activities. Try to fit a soothing bath in there, too, and you should feel strong and well enough to tackle your duties.

Stomach

I've spoken of indigestion and gas in the stomach, but if you have a recurring condition, you may need an amulet to ward off the severity of attacks. First, be sure you try teas of strawberry, thyme, and wild cherry which are very good for cases of indigestion, and then make yourself an amulet of red satin (sew into a sack). Put into your sack a red rose, a charm made in the form of a heart and enameled red, and a silver earring worn by gypsies. (You may have to visit a gypsy for that one and pay a pretty penny for it, but it's worth it to complete the charm against stomach trouble). Once you have the amulet on, wear it for forty-eight hours, whether or not your stomach problems have gone away. At the end of the time, burn the red rose in a dish, then scatter the ashes at a crossroads at midnight. While doing this, chant: ''Pain to rose, rose ashes to dust. Keep me free, oh God, from illness of the stomach.'' The next time you have a severe attack, take out your amulet and repeat the process.

Swellings

If you have a swelling and you want to make it go down, try ice. If that doesn't work, then try a poultice of fenugreek, mugwort, or yellow dock. Wear an amulet of the braided hairs from a horse and hang on it a charm that you're especially fond of. It could be anything. Chant over the charm: "Sickness stay away with my _____" (and name the amulet object). Wear it till the swelling has disappeared.

Tobacco

I've mentioned smoking elsewhere, but I want to be sure that you have the proper amulet and remedy to combat it. When you are just overwhelmed with craving as you give up smoking, peppermint tea is an excellent home remedy to use. Vervain also is effective, and burdock is a cleansing agent which will help rid the tobacco from your bloodstream. While you're going through all of this torture—and it is—you will need assistance of some kind. Go to a smoker's group, for instance, and try not to eat candy as it only leads to another addiction—sweets. If you carry the amulet I recommend, it should cut short the period when you are critical. Put into a brown satin sack a smoked cigarette butt, a small silver salt or demitasse spoon, and a red carnation blossom. Chant over the amulet as you make it: "Keep my body free and full of health. Away cigarettes." When you finally begin to feel more confident about not smoking, bury the butt from the amulet in the ground, about a foot down, and cover it with leaves (no special kind).

Tonics

You've read a lot about tonics for the blood, but it doesn't hurt for me to recommend a few more plus a holistic amulet. Chamomile is the number one tonic, blood cleanser, and nerve-soothing remedy. Take several cups and see how much better you feel. Coriander makes another good tea for a tonic, and sassafras is also excellent. Take a piece of Saran Wrap and wind in it some pepper, some skullcap, and a picture of yourself in a golden heart. If it's a baby picture, so much the better. Carry the amulet around in your pocket for a few days, then empty the pepper in the back garden and say over it: ''Clean my body, impurities to the ground.'' You should feel much better having gone through this process and you'll be able to be very alert and with a lot of energy.

Tonsillitis

An effective remedy for tonsillitis or a subsequent tonsillectomy is tansy. What you do first is gargle with it, then take a swallow. Tansy will soothe your throat which is bound to hurt for awhile from the surgery. Before you take any healing remedies for your throat, however, get your doctor's approval. Sometimes antibiotics don't agree with home remedies and you have to stop taking the latter. For all operations, keep a sack of blue velvet (dark blue) and into it put an unset piece of turquoise stone, a silver charm of a person, and a seashell. If you're American Indian, add to the bag a thunderbird. Wear this amulet whenever an illness comes or you have to be operated on. Your surgery will go smoothly and your illness will heal more quickly than if you didn't have it on.

Vaginal Remedies

It's a good idea to take a douche now and then to keep that area of your body clean. The best douches are the ones prescribed by doctors that are made of salt or other substances that they recommend. But other good douches are made of fennel, slippery elm, and white pond lily. You can prepare these yourself by boiling the plants and then letting them cool into a comfortable douche. If you have other more serious vaginal problems, you'll need to carry an amulet. Into a red satin sack put a dried sweet pea, a picture of the Virgin Mary, and a touch of marshmallow (a plant). When your vaginal troubles have abated, plant the herbs and flower in a garden by a white picket fence (could be a neighbor's), and chant: ''Sickness away to haunt the earth.'' You should start feeling much freer of the vaginal troubles you've been having.

Varicose Veins

You're going to need poultices for a case of varicose veins. They're so ugly and uncomfortable that you'll need to treat them regularly. Make a poultice of witch hazel or bayberry bark or white oak bark. Let your legs soak in the poultice which should be the result of boiling the barks and wrapping your limb with the liquid you made from them. You'll also need an amulet to help you through the period when the unsightly veins are really visible. Take a silver chain purse (you can find them in antique stores) and put in it a newly minted penny, several dried rose hips, and a penknife. Chant over the charm: ''Keep my veins from aching and showing through my skin.'' Then wear the amulet for a week. It seems to me that you should have an operation on the veins if they're that bad. But if they're just showing through your skin a little bit, then the amulet and poultices should work nicely.